GLOUCESTERSHIRE
&
FOREST OF DEAN
WALKS

BOOK ONE

by

John Abbott

Published by
REARDON & SON
Publishers
56, Upper Norwood Street, Leckhampton,
CHELTENHAM, GLOS, GL53 ODU

Copyright c 1996
REARDON & SON

Written and researched
by
John Abbott

Cover Design
by
Peter Reardon

ISBN 1 873877 14 5

Photography by David Medcroft.
and thanks to the Stewarts for their support.

Printed
by
PHILIPRINT
CHELTENHAM, GLOS.

CONTENTS

INTRODUCTION

This book describes ten walks in glorious Gloucestershire. It covers an area south-west of the M50 and M5, from Tewkesbury to Ruardean.

The theme is history; village churches, in particular with, where necessary, a description of the main features. Other places of interest to walker and visitor alike are also mentioned, for example: Tewkesbury's Abbey and alleys; the Cathedral, Beatrix Potter Museum and docks in Gloucester.

A sketch map is included with each walk, though these are no substitute for the Ordnance Survey maps of the area. Their Landranger and Pathfinder series give a clear picture of the terrain to be covered.

Many of the walks include long/short options and range from easy to quite demanding - an easy mile at Ashleworth - up to ten miles around Newent and Upleadon; enough, hopefully, to satisfy most people.

If you are new to walking, like any activity, it is wise to pace yourself, building stamina as you progress. Dress sensibly. Pack a waterproof - weather forecasts have been known to be wrong. Boots that have been worn a few times, proven 'blister free', are recommended. Woollen socks are a good idea, as well.

Respect the countryside: guard against risk of fire; stay on the paths; keep fido under control; do not disturb livestock; close gates (unless obviously meant to be open); avoid damage to crops, fences, hedges, trees and so on; leave no litter; and take care of yourself, especially along roads, using the grass verge wherever possible.

I apologise in advance should you find that a walk does not correspond with my description. While every care has been taken in the compilation of this book, the author cannot accept responsibility for any errors. Furthermore, you may have to cope with the sticky clay of freshly ploughed fields, waist-high crops, new stiles, gates, fences, even a change of route - anything can happen, and sometimes does. Church and other detail, too, can change.

Unfortunately, it is not easy (sometimes impossible) to get to the start of a walk and home again without some form of transport of your own. The problem is that many of today's bus routes in the country are privately run - operators and times may vary from year to year. One useful publication, 'liberated' from a TIC, is Connections, which contains bus and train timetables for the Forest of Dean. Although 'floaters' might disagree, walking is the best exercise that you can get; so whether you intend to wander for half an hour or trek for four - walk the good walk and, above all, enjoy yourself.

I have added two general articles at the end: one on the Church; the other, to be taken with a pinch of leather wax, rambles on about the possible problems encountered en route.

TEWKESBURY - TOWN AND COUNTRY

Tewkesbury attracts thousands of visitors every year; in addition to a fine Abbey, the town still retains a medieval flavour, with many centuries-old, even timber-framed, houses lining its three main streets. Restricted by the Rivers Avon and Severn, the seventeenth century needs of an increasing population were met by new housing, often several storeys high, packed in behind the main thoroughfares. This resulted in a maze of narrow alleys and courts: little more than collectors of rubbish and glorified drains in those times; and one of Tewkesbury's many delights today.

Town and Country ... after a look at the Abbey, you have a choice of two walks. The first is within the town itself - a mix of paths and pavements - across the Severn Ham, by the Mill Avon, window-shopping the streets and up and down three alleys, though you may sample many more. The second walk takes you alongside the River Severn to Deerhurst. You will visit a Saxon chapel, a Saxon church, and 'see action' along part of the Battle Trail.

The Battle of Tewkesbury was one of most important battles of the Wars of the Roses. It took place on Saturday, 4th May, 1471 and ended in defeat for the Lancastrians. Many of the Lancastrian nobility were killed, including the Prince of Wales who lies buried in the Abbey Choir. The Battle Trail 'commemorates' the event. Battle Waymark Signs define a walk through the general battlefield area.

Route: *Tewkesbury - Deerhurst - Tewkesbury.*
Distance/Time: *I have broken the 'walk' down into: a browse of any length of time around around the Abbey; a stroll of one hour through the town; five miles through the country.*
Map: *O.S. Landranger 150.*
Start: *See Parking.*
Terrain: *Good. Virtually level all the way with only a modicum of mud and the odd nettle.*
Nearest Towns: *Worcester, Gloucester, Cheltenham, Cirencester.*
Access: *Make for junction 9 of the M5; from there, the Abbey is extremely well signposted.*
Parking: *Turning left off Church Street along Gander Lane, you have a choice of the Abbey Park on your right or the Long Stay Park a bit further on to your left. The former is best, providing you get there early.*
Public Transport: *Ring Gloucester County Council on 01 452 425543.*
Refreshments: *Food and drink are everywhere, at a price. A cheaper option, weather permitting, is to have a picnic. There is a patch of grass with seating beside the Long Stay Park. Choose the right day and you could even watch the cricket, nearby.*

Public Toilets: *By the Abbey Park or near Yarnell's Alley, mentioned en route. The Abbey:*
For information: *times of services, music, the Abbey House and so forth, ring the Abbey Office on 01 684 850959.*
The Tourist Office: At 64 Barton Street. Telephone: 01 684 295027.

Tewkesbury Abbey

TEWKESBURY ABBEY

There are books available from the Abbey Shop that tell you all you need to know regarding the history and fabric of the Abbey. By way of an appetiser, a brief description from yours truly follows. How brief is brief? How difficult it is to extract the essential for what is really just a walking article. A full account would require a book of doormat proportions.

Tewkesbury Abbey was founded by the Norman nobleman, Robert FitzHamon, who died in 1107. His tomb lies in the Founder's Chantry (or chapel) within the Abbey. The building continued - the Abbey was consecrated in 1121; one can easily see how its enormous tower dominates the town.

First, getting there: from either car park [see *Parking*], go west towards the Abbey, along the path to the north porch. Approaching, one gets a much better view of the tower - twelfth century - topped with battlements, pinnacles and a golden rooster. Services are held, usually early in the day, when you may not be allowed in; a notice in the porch advises. If this proves to be the case, why not do the town walk which is described later? It ends in Gander Lane which bisects the two car parks. Assuming all is well, go through the north porch and around to the right, where you will find a table stacked with leaflets. The 'Welcome to Tewkesbury Abbey' leaflet is a useful guide.

You may, of course, choose your own route; mine starts at the leaflets and goes east along the north aisle in a clockwise direction. Again, this is merely a summary, touching the vaulted high spots. There is much to see - too much, almost; most of which is described, anyway, in the form of notices by each feature. So, taking a deep breath, and with apologies for any mistakes - looking to left and right ...

A Gurney Stove: originally burning cheap anthracite, now converted to gas. If you have any used stamps or unwanted spectacles conveniently to hand - not in the stove - in the collection point along the north wall. An effigy set in the north wall. Another Gurney Stove. In the north transept, the Grove Organ, built in 1885 and presented to the Abbey by the Reverend Charles Grove. A seventeenth century strong box. The Abbey Shop - a prolonged browse, here. Continuing - the fifteenth century Warwick or Beauchamp Chapel. The aforementioned Founder's Chantry, containing the tomb of the founder of Tewkesbury Abbey, Robert FitzHamon. The Chapel of St Margaret, Queen of Scotland. The Despenser Tomb. The Chapels of St Edmund and St Dunstan - born near Glastonbury in the early part of the tenth century, St Dunstan contributed much to the art of bellfounding. Campanologists will recognise him as the Patron Saint of Bell Ringers.

Around the ambulatory at the east end, the fifteenth century Wakeman Cenotaph, depicting a decaying cadaver. A nearby grating, under which lies the vault of George, Duke of Clarence who, by all accounts, was drowned in a butt of Malmsey wine. And a striking 'metal sculpture' of 'Our Lady Queen of Peace'. An adjacent notice describes the Lady Chapel, destroyed in 1540. In the south-west corner, the Robeson Cenotaph, the Chapel of St Faith, and the Chapel of St John the Baptist and St Catherine.

Tombs - walking west along the south aisle: Hugh le Despenser, hanged in 1325; Richard Cheltenham, Abbot of Tewkesbury in the fifteenth century; Robert Forthington, Abbot of Tewkesbury in the thirteenth century; the Chapel of Edward, Baron le Despenser; and the tomb of Alan, Abbot of Tewkesbury in the twelfth century, and Thomas Becket's biographer. In the south transept, with a stand for votive candles, the Lady Chapel; a chandelier hangs here.

Tewkesbury Town

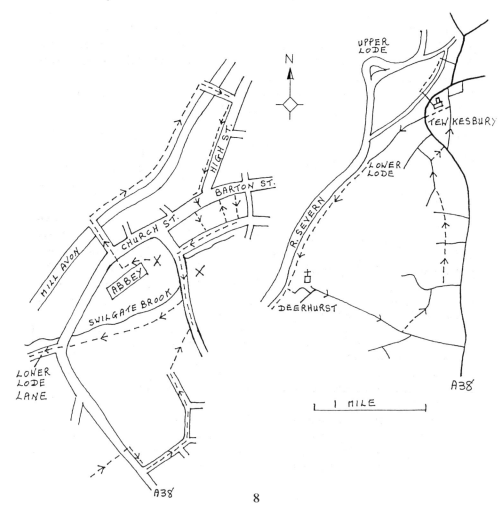

8

Now go right into the choir, pulling out the stops, walking up the steps for a closer look at the Milton Organ - back down and on to the high altar. See the small brasses set in the floor, the red and blue of the fourteenth century choir vaulting, high above, and the seven stained glass windows, also dating from the fourteenth century. Returning to the nave - on your right, stands a smaller third organ, presented to Tewkesbury Abbey by Colonel H N Thoyts in 1918.

Continue west along the south aisle, passing the font and coming to the Holy Cross Chapel in the south-west corner. Finally, back at the leaflets, pause and look east, along the nave, with massive columns on either side, vaulting above, through to the choir - an impressive sight. Why not go around a second time; anticlockwise, for a change?

Leaving via the north porch, one may go left and left again, through a gate (sometimes locked) by the Abbey House, walking around the outside of the Abbey.

Did you get a copy of: 'Music in the Abbey'? There is a full and varied programme of music throughout the year. Also a copy of: 'Summer events at the Abbey House'? A chance to see the sixteenth century Abbot's Parlour, enjoy an evening recital, and even take tea in the parlour itself.

THE WALK

Standing, once more, outside the north porch, it is time to start the town part of the walk. Proceed north to Church Street - the busy A38. Cross with care to Mill Street, opposite; past the Millcot Gallery as far as the Abbey Mill Restaurant. Take the path just to the right of the restaurant - over the Abbey Mill Sluice that straddles the Mill Avon to Severn Ham.

Bear right, north-east, walking along the river bank - you will see many boats and a few barges moored. Further on, right, again, over the bridge, direction east, and then left, down to Healings Mill. Currently, the area is the subject of a preservation order. Now go right along Quay Street - fancy a quick snack? A bag of chips from Kingsfisher Ltd. Read the two notices on the wall while waiting - a layman's guide to potatoes and fish, the latter in several languages. Quay Street ends at High Street.

Right, here, along the pavement - there are many old houses on both sides of the street, some timber-framed. To mention a few in passing: the sixteenth century Nottingham Arms; the fifteenth century Ancient Grudge Hotel; Clarence House, which has origins back in the fourteenth century. There are many alleys, too; by now, you should have passed Wilkes Alley - did you notice it? Very narrow, as they all are. Continue to just beyond the War Memorial and take the pedestrian crossing, which brings you to the Berkeley Arms. A door with the words: 'home cooked food and accommodation' above it, if open, will lead you to a medieval barn, which may be viewed with permission.

And now for three alleys: at the Berkeley Arms, go right a few yards and then left into Lilley's Alley (the sign is above your head as you enter), past the timber-framed Tudor Cottage and Claypipes (mind your head). Bear left along Swilgate Road, past The Bolt Hole, Compton's Alley and Fletcher's Alley. Then left into Hughes Alley - watch for the sign on the wall, it is easily missed. There is a bend in the alley, its purpose being to reduce the tunnelling effect of the wind. Now go right along Barton Street, past Fish Alley, and right into Yarnell's Alley, which ends at Saffron Road. *You may care to take advantage of the public toilets, which are just around to the left*. Turn right down narrow Saffron Road and right, again, retracing your steps along Swilgate Road to Gander Lane and the car parks. So ends the town walk, a stroll of no more than an hour. If you want to really stretch your legs, why not continue with five miles through the country?

At Gander Lane, bear left and then right across the sports ground, direction south-west, keeping the Swilgate Brook to your right; incidentally, joining the Battle Trail. There are fine views of the Abbey Church and tower on your right. You pass two posts with yellow arrow-heads and come to a gate and the still busy A38. Cross with even more care, taking the road opposite - Lower Lode Lane - direction west. Further on, you leave the signposted Battle Trail (to rejoin later), and continue down Lower Lode Lane, now part of the Severn Way Path. At Lower Lode, where the Avon meets the Severn, go on past the boat house - see the floodmark on the wall - 1947 was a good year for ducks.

The path tracks alongside the River Severn; a stretch of mostly pleasant, level walking. Mostly means a spot of mud with a seasonal sting in its tail - nettles in the late spring - and a scattering of dock leaves, just in case. You come to a gate and blue arrow-head - see the Church of St Mary, Deerhurst, in the distance. Another gate, and along beyond the line of the church - the path veers left, away from the river to a signpost. Left, here, south-east, squeezing by a gate to the road, and around to Odda's Chapel.

A notice advises: '... built by Odda in memory of his brother Elfric and dedicated in 1056 ...' Only a few years before the Norman Conquest: a simple Saxon chapel ... nave and chancel ... and an inscribed tablet.

At the road, turn right, on to the Priory Church of St Mary, Deerhurst. The church has origins back as far as the ninth century and was restored in the tenth century after the Viking invasions. Inside, there is a wealth of literature available which describes the church much better than I. Also, a glass display case which holds, among other items: a Roman coin, a pair of lampwick trimmers and shot, possibly dating from the Battle of Tewkesbury. On your left, in the north-west corner, stands the ninth century font. The bowl was rescued from a farmyard by Bishop Wilberforce in the nineteenth century. Walking along the north aisle brings you to the two Cassey brasses - Sir John and Dame Alice, and also two other brasses of Ladies. Brass rubbers may apply for permission at Priory Farm.

Around to the pulpit - nineteenth century - twelve panels of carved wood; and the sanctuary with seating on three sides and the Ten Commandments on the east wall. In the south-east corner are replicas of the two Cassey brasses. A notice advises that Sir John, who died in 1400, was the Chief Baron of the Exchequer to King Richard II. Dame Alice's dog lies at her feet; uniquely, its name, 'Terri', is recorded on the brass. On leaving the church, you may wish to see the angel - follow the signs around to your right.

Bear left at the road, direction east, walking to a T-junction. Again, left, signposted Tewkesbury, around by the entrance to Priory Farm, and along - a straight stretch of road - passing Barn Cottage and Grove Barn, ignoring the bridleway just beyond. Approaching the B4213, take the bridleway, left, north-east. A shade muddy in wet weather, it ascends slightly (one of only two very modest ascents during the walk) and joins a narrow road. Go straight on, and then right at the junction. You come to a signposted footpath on your left, direction north. The sign 'Southwick Farm' is on the fence. Over the cattle grid ... the lane is stony underfoot, bears left and joins another lane, surfaced, this time, where a signpost points right, resuming a northerly direction. Continue, and where the lane bears right, go straight ahead, past a washing line. Further on, you will see a yellow arrow-head on a post - walking along the edge of a field, now, the path passes through a gap in the hedge - but ignore, still keeping the hedge to your right. At the end of the field, yet another arrow-head directs around to a 'metal' stile and the road which leads to Southwick Park.

Devil-face keystone, St. John the Baptist, Chaceley

Proceed through a gap in the railings opposite, and up a field (the second modest ascent). Currently, there is very long grass and the path is none too clear - just keep north - finally passing between a bungalow and a house and taking the stile opposite. A field and then a stile on your left brings you to the road, where you bear right, north, again. Ahead, a signpost points right, east, passing close to Crosslands - and so do you - off the tarmac drive, over a fence with an attempt at a step at its base - soon walking north-east, across an often muddy patch of ground, rejoining the Battle Trail. Continue north-east along the field - new housing on your left will probably spread to the field in a few years.

At the eternally busy A38, cross to the pavement and turn right. It is Battle Trail the rest of the way - left into Abbot's road - left along Abbot's walk - the path beside the cemetery to the park - finally joining Gander Lane, back to the start of the walk.

FORTHAMPTON AND CHACELEY

One could say that this is a rather unusual walk; for in addition to providing an hour or two of healthy exercise in glorious Gloucestershire, it intrudes, punishes, and is lashings of fun. A contradiction? Well, the walk is intrusive in the sense that it briefly encroaches upon foreign territory - Hereford and Worcester, and historically punishing in terms of village stocks. Offbeat, too; a whipping post furnishes lashings of fun.

Route: *Forthampton - Chaceley - Forthampton.*
Distance: *About five miles.*
Map: *O.S. Landranger 150*
Start: *See Parking*
Terrain: *Generally level with a dash of mud in wet weather.*
Nearest Towns: *Tewkesbury, Worcester, Gloucester, Cheltenham, Cirencester.*
Access: *Make for junction 9 of the M5. From there, take the A438 through Tewkesbury, bearing right at the roundabout centred on the War Memorial - A438 and A38 - to where you turn left along the A438, the Ledbury road. Forthampton is about two miles further on, signposted to your left, though the sign is small with lettering that is none too easy to read. The village sign Long Green is a few yards beyond. Forthampton is at map ref: 858325.*
Parking: *Entering Forthampton, go left at the crossroads. You can park on the grass verge opposite the church or beside the village hall in Church Lane.*
Public Transport: *Ring Gloucester County Council on 01 452 425543.*
Refreshments: *Forthampton Shop and Post Office is passed conveniently near the end of the walk and sells nuts, fruit, chocolate and so forth; even non-edible stamps for the postcard that you may have bought in the church. It is closed on Wednesday and Saturday afternoons and Sundays.*

Having parked [*see Parking*], make for the Church of St Mary, Forthampton. With origins in the thirteenth century, St Mary's has undergone many additions and alterations in the succeeding years. Take the main entrance to the churchyard. On your left, you will see the village stocks and a whipping post: punishment, indeed; certainly no slapped wrist for the delinquents of not so long ago. Near the south porch, again on your left, stands a seventeenth century pedestal and sundial - much worn, looking its age.

Inside, the light switches are to your right; preferably used sparingly and switched off before you leave (as I was politely advised). The ornate font is nineteenth century. Immediately to your left, on the south wall, is a reredos - formerly the screen behind the altar - showing Christ and two disciples. Further along the south wall, inscribed on a brass plate, you can read Matthew's Song. The columns and arches of a nineteenth century arcade run along the north side. Walking east down the north aisle - a Visitors' Book is there for signing (you may even buy a pen). Postcards are also for sale; intriguingly, see Refreshments should you need a stamp. Entering the chancel - a rare thirteenth century stone altar - the light shining through stained glass of the east window looks particularly attractive. Returning along the south side - above one of the columns of the arcade is a tablet to John Rasteil - you can read the date, an old-style 1631, and see a skeleton (carved, not real) in the lower part of the tablet.

Forthampton and Chaceley

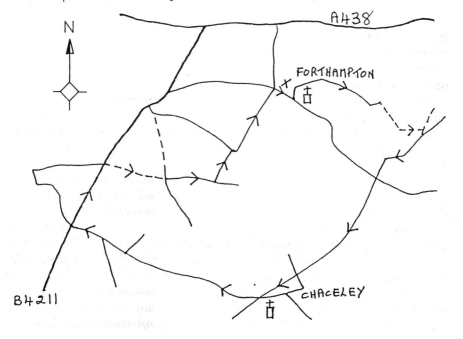

THE WALK

Return to the road and go right along Church Lane - past the village hall and Alcock's Farm - the lane loses its surface - walking south-east, coming eventually to a gate. It is well-secured but persevere. On across a field, keeping the hedge to your left, to a post and yellow arrow-head. Pause here to take a bearing - south-south-east, give or take a degree. Continue; on your left you can see what has to be the tower of Tewkesbury Abbey in the distance. The bearing should have brought you to a right angle of hedge, about three-quarters of the way along the field. Up and over the stile in the corner (careful, it can be slippery), veering left slightly, down a pasture to a gate and stile. Over, striking roughly east - a field to a track - turning right, passing to the right of Home Farm, going right, south-west, along the metalled lane to the crossroads, and then straight across, signposted Chaceley and Gloucester. A walk of a mile or so, passing smoky Woodbine Cottage and the DIY sign of Vicarage Field Farm, entering the village of Chaceley. The small spire of the Church of St John the Baptist is visible, ahead.

Proceed through the churchyard and around to the south porch. The 'Churches around Tewkesbury' leaflet advises: if locked, keys may be obtained from Grain House Farm, opposite. Dating from the twelfth century, St John's was mostly rebuilt in the fourteenth century. The tower and spire are thirteenth and fourteenth century. Inside, on your right - more punishment - village stocks on the floor. In the corner, past the piscina set in the south wall, stands an old drum. According to the 'bat' which hangs on a hook on one of the columns, the drum was formerly one of the instruments of the church orchestra and accompanied the singing before an organ was installed. Pass under an arch of the arcade - sculptured corbel heads (that need a hair cut) stare down from both sides. Walking east, along the north side - see the devil-face keystone in the Norman chancel arch; smiling, archly, I think. On through the choir - high in the centre of the east window - fourteenth century stained glass depicting the Crucifixion. Also in the chancel you will see another piscina in the south wall and a fourteenth century double aumbry (a recess for church vessels) in the east wall.

Leaving the church, go right this time, through the gate to the road. Bear left, then almost immediately right, signposted Corse Lawn. A long stretch of narrow road, past Lawn Farm (no reps), to the B4211. Thou shalt not trespass - but you have, into Hereford and Worcester. Right, here; the traffic presents no problem, for one may walk along the adjoining field. Continue to the narrow grass verge, as far as the telephone box on the opposite side of the road. Again, right - a bridleway, initially a lane, which soon becomes uneven underfoot and is quite muddy in places. Straight across at the 'path crossroads', passing a blue arrow-head on a post. You come to an unsurfaced lane and a signpost - three choices - three white walkers among the greenery. Follow the one that points left, north-east, and at the road, go right - it curves sharply to the left, a modest ascent, the road levels - a small pond, a barn, a larger pond - an equally modest descent, and then right at the crossroads, signposted Lower Lode, Chaceley and Tirley. The War Memorial is on the corner. Opposite Corner House Farm is yet another pond. No zebras, just a notice: 'PLEASE BEWARE DUCKS CROSSING'. Look carefully, and if all is well, continue, back to the start of the walk.

STAUNTON AND TIRLEY

Here, I offer a choice - walker's, not Hobson's - the long or short option. There are also options within options, where soft and hard translate to easy and not so easy. There is even a cider option. Rolling English roads: the long option is roughly oval-shaped - it starts at St Michael's Church, Tirley, bounces along the border of Hereford and Worcester, tumbles close to Staunton and returns. The Church of St James near Staunton is not visited, the reason being that it is kept locked and keys are at a house that lies a good mile away. St Michael's more than compensates. The short option has the same beginning and end but prunes the oval to a circle of sorts, cutting south at the B4211, passing through Tirley Knowle and joining the longer route near Tirley Court.

Route: *Tirley - Staunton - Tirley.*
Distance: *About four or eight miles.*
Map: *O.S. Landranger 150.*
Start: *See Parking.*
Terrain: *Mostly level, though possibly muddy and overgrown in places.*
Nearest Towns: *Worcester, Tewkesbury, Gloucester.*
Access: *From the north: junction 9 of the M5, A438 to Tewkesbury, A38 and B4213, passing the Tirley village sign and taking the road on your right, signposted Chaceley and Forthampton. From the south: junction 11 of the M5 (round the roundabouts around Gloucester), A40, A38 and B4213, as before. Returning from the B4213 to the A38 and going right, can be difficult in traffic.*
Parking: *On the patch of grass beside St Michael's Church, Tirley.*
Public Transport: *Ring Gloucester County Council on 01 452 425543. There is a bus shelter near the Tirley crossroads.*
Refreshments: *At the crossroads that lead to the church, go left, south-east, along the B4213 to Haw Bridge. A walk or drive of about half a mile. As well as enjoying the views across the River Severn, one may sup in the Haw Bridge Inn on one side or the New Inn (no motorcycles) on the other. Recent history: the bridge was opened on 29th September, 1961, by His Grace the Duke of Beaufort.*

'Grassily' parked [see *Access and Parking*], recently rendered St Michael's stands ready and waiting. With origins in the thirteenth century, though now mostly fourteenth and fifteenth century, St Michael's was restored in 1894 and underwent a further restoration of its exterior in 1986. Currently, the gate to the

15

churchyard has a hinge problem - that overcome, look up at the tower - battlemented, with a pinnacle at each corner. The white face of the clock on the south wall catches the eye; it was made from the end of a beer barrel. The clockface was repainted during the 1986 restoration. The clock itself, was built by John Carter, a wheel-wright. A real DIY masterpiece - no parts from other clocks were used. He adapted, for example, a bicycle pedal, a scythe, a cannonball, the barrel of a pistol - and it is still working, today. According to the booklet, the clock was installed in 1918 as a memorial to Second-lieutenant George Edward Fowler of the Twelfth Battalion Gloucestershire Regiment, who was killed in action near Ypres in 1917.

Barrel face of clock (detail), St.Michael, Tirley

Enter via the timber-framed south porch. Immediately to your right, set in the south wall, is a stoup for holy water. Somewhat low, you might think; virtually at floor level. The floor has been raised over the years due to flooding of the River Severn. On your left is a Visitors' Book and a booklet by B.E. Pegler, giving a history of the church and parish. Further on your left, on the sill of the window, are several framed photographs: the church during the 1990 flood, the clock mechanism and more reading material. You may also hear the occasional 'chunky' tick of the clock. The Norman font is tub-shaped. Alongside the north wall, standing on trestles, is an ancient chest with the usual three locks requiring the presence of the Vicar and two churchwardens before it could be opened. A model of the church rests on top.

Walking east along the nave - the hanging oil lamps are Victorian. In the north wall are three stained glass windows to the memory of the Hone family. Joseph Hone was the Vicar of Tirley for sixty years. You can read the dedications at their base. Approaching the chancel - the arch is thirteenth century - look up and see the 'remains' of a wall painting - fading blues, browns and reds - early sixteenth century. On one side of the chancel arch are two plates marking the 1947 and 1990 flood levels. In 1947, one could have swum along the nave! Entering the chancel - in the south-east corner is a trefoil-headed piscina, again almost at floor level. The east window, behind the altar, dates from 1873, and is in memory of William Browne. To its right, is an icon of the Archangel Michael.

THE WALK

Back at the road, it is time to exercise one's options - decisions - long or short, or both? It is up to you. As previously mentioned, both options are the same at the beginning and end. I will describe the shorter one first, noting where the longer section leaves and joins, and 'slot it in' later.

Turn right, direction north - in early autumn, the blackberries are not quite ready for eating, mostly greens and reds. Continue to Town St. Farm (recommended by the English Tourist Board). Why not invest in B & B for a couple of days and really explore the area? Just beyond the farm, where the road goes right, bear left, north-west.

Staunton and Tirley

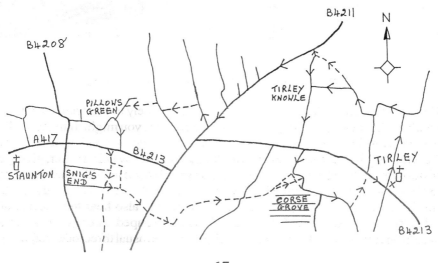

17

I MILE

The road ascends, levels and curves right, signposted Tirley Knowle and Corse Lawn (sounding like a gardener's nightmare), to a point a few yards beyond Little Sandpits Farm. Two choices: easy and not so easy. More easily, continue straight ahead, passing LSF's bigger brother, to the T-junction at Tirley Knowle. This is where the long option walk bears right, to the B4211. Not so easily, take the narrow road, right, just beyond Little Sandpits Farm. The hard surface leads around to the entrance of a house, so continue straight ahead along grass, direction north-west. A path-cum-bridleway which, according to the time of year, can be very muddy and full of brambles and nettles; quite heavy going. The path ends at the road. As before, the long option walk bears right, to the B4211. Naturally enough, the short option walk bears left, passing the T-junction, where your alter ego has been waiting, rested, unscratched and mud-free, at Tirley Knowle. Here, proceed south-west, signposted Tirley, passing Rose Tree Cottage with its high conifer hedge, and Knowle Farm. A longish stretch to the B4213.

Cross with care and turn left, then after fifty yards or so, go right, south-west, signposted Tirley. Negotiate three bends in the road. The first passes the entrance to Tirley Court, the second is joined on your right by the long option walk - a path across a field. Forever onward, ignoring the road to your right, and the signed footpath that points, impossibly, through dense undergrowth. Beyond a farm, the road descends to a spot opposite Netherstone Cottage, where you will see another signed footpath on your left. Up and over (careful, it is a high one and partly covered in grass), walking north-east across a field. Currently, a crop is growing, and though passable, the field is somewhat sticky underfoot. You can see the tower of Tirley's church in the distance. The stile at the end leads to a lane where an arrow-head directs, again to the B4213. Cross to the pavement and bear right as far as the crossroads, where you go left, signposted Chaceley and Forthampton, back to the start of the walk. A doddle; don't you wish that you had taken the long way around? The next time, perhaps.

And so to the long option: it continues from where the Tirley Knowle road meets the B4211 (at approximate map ref: 829304). Cross and turn left, signposted Gloucester, walking along a field's width of grass verge. Wandering, nibbling sheep are everywhere - and further along, on the opposite side, an old milestone: 'Eldersfield Upton 8, Gloster 8'. The road curves left, slightly - on past a cattle sign, still 'grass-verging', soon taking the second right, signposted Lime Street, to a signed footpath on your left.

This gate has to be climbed. You will see a yellow arrow-head with the words: 'Whitmore Way' and a pair of 'bootprints'. Over and along, direction west, across a footbridge - a field - through a gap in the hedge - a touch of tarmac, still west, to the road. Turn right, a mere yard or ten, to another signed footpath on your left. A double gate, a lane, a second double gate, and then across a field, close to a line of telegraph poles to a stile and metalled lane. Bear left, and at the junction, left, again, along sleepy Pillows Green Road to the B4213. Here, go right, watching for approaching traffic, and crossing to the signed footpath opposite. The Whitmore arrow-head points across a footbridge, direction south, to a gate which is opened with difficulty. Continue south: a succession of fields and stiles; currently, just beyond and to the left of the penultimate stile is a DIY gate with binder twine hinges. This is where you go left, direction south-east, confidently taking in your stride more stiles, fields and a footbridge to the B4211. First, you may wish to continue to the last stile - in the hedge, further along on to your right. A plaque on the other side reads: 'Erected in memory of John Thomas Whitmore, 1944-1987...' Hence, the Whitmore Way. The road west leads to Snig's End and the Chartist Houses, part of a community founded in the mid-nineteenth century by Fergus O'Connor. Four acres and basic accommodation - living-room, kitchen and bedroom. Due to alterations/extensions and so forth, they have since changed out of all recognition.

Cross the B4211 with care, taking the stile opposite, along a field, approaching the only ascent of the walk - a stiff climb to the top of Corse Wood Hill. In wet weather, the ground 'inclines' to be slippery. At the top, nimbly leap over the stile in the corner, walking east-north-east, making for a water trough in the distance. An arrow-head on a post is close by. Continue east - two more stiles - standing on the second, and sighting north-east, you should see the vague outline of a white disc on a post. Ignore, forging forever east, with the hedge to your right - grass and thistles - to yet another stile in the corner. Over and left, to - yes - a stile, then along the field, still east, to the road.

Here, go left a few yards and on through the gate opposite (a nifty reef knot is required). A long field, this - to the far right-hand corner - a rickety stile - an arrow-head on a post - eternally east along rough ground. Corse Grove is to your right. At the hedge, follow the strip of grass around left, north-east, to a gap in the hedge and a post clothed in arrow-heads. Here, take the path straight across the field, direction north-east, which should (hopefully) bring you to a signpost and stile - and there you are: turning right, joining the short option walk back to Tirley.

PAUNTLEY AND REDMARLEY

Traditional Christmas entertainment at any time of the year. A walking pantomime - with optional cat and mayoral potential - around Pauntley Court, where Pauntley Manor, the birthplace of Dick Whittington once stood. A look at two churches and a stroll through the Leadon Vale. Did the mayor-to-be do this walk with his black cat in preparation for his trek to London, I wonder?

Route: Pauntley - Redmarley - Pauntley.
Distance: About five miles.
Map: O.S. Landranger 150.
Start: See Parking.

Terrain: Good, apart from a dash of red mud.
Nearest Towns: Worcester, Tewkesbury, Gloucester.
Access: Pauntley church is at map ref: 749289. I prefer to go the long way around: junction 8 of the M5, junction 2 of the M50 and then along the A417, the Gloucester road.
Passing the Redmarley D'Abitot village sign, take the second right, signposted Redmarley and Newent. There is another sharp right at Playley Green, signposted Redmarley and Newent, where you continue past the sign: 'Redmarley - drive carefully through the village'. Follow the road around left at the War Memorial, passing Redmarley church (parking here is awkward, hence the base of Pauntley), again veering left, signposted Redmarley and Newent. The road descends, crosses the River Leadon (a part of this is walked), passes the Pauntley village sign, ascends and levels. From here, drive slowly, looking for a sign on your left to Pauntley Court: 'Birthplace of Dick Whittington 1358 - 1423. Three times Lord Mayor of London'.
Parking: Turning left down this lane brings you to the church. In front, conveniently, is a patch of grass for the car.
Public Transport: Ring Gloucester County Council on 01 452 425543.
Refreshments: Bring a flask.

What's in a name? Pauntley lies in the Hundred of Botloe. The village of Redmarley D'Abitot is also included in the walk. Unusual names, obscure locations: Pauntley, in particular, is not the easiest of places to find. Boots at the ready, I assume that you are standing outside the Church of St John the Evangelist, Pauntley [see *Access and Parking*]. A visit before the walk seems appropriate.

St John's dates from the twelfth century. Entering the churchyard, look up at the battlements and gargoyles that top the tower, and then walk around to the south side to admire the twelfth century Norman doorway. You will see a fish scale tympanum (which may have interested Dick's cat) between the chevron arch and lintel. It is too early for a rest, but on your right is a seat - a quiet and pleasant spot to sit at the end of the walk, weather permitting.

Back at the timbered north porch - you may have trouble opening the door - a quick flick of the wrist is necessary. Inside, the font is to your right, and opposite, on the south side, a Visitors' Book for signing. There is also a booklet for purchasing that describes the church, Dick Whittington (fact and fiction) and the history of the area. Walking east along the nave - the Norman chancel arch is double-chevroned. Inside the chancel, to your right, hangs a notice describing the Assistant Priests' Stall: '... presented by the Corporation of London ... in memory of Dick Whittington...' The fourteenth century stained glass at the top of the window in the north wall depicts several shields of arms, including the Whittington Arms. Below, is a framed copy of his election as Mayor of London and a small carved wooden figure of Christ. Two Jacobean chairs stand one on

20

either side of the altar. Turning right, into the St George's Chapel: a thirteenth century pillar piscina stands behind a glass case which contains the Bible. On the left is a brass to William Pauncefoote (1616), and on the right another to Elizabeth Pole (1543). Further on the right is a marble monument to Anne Somerset: 'Died 4th March 1764 aged 70.' Beneath are inscriptions to her sister and nephew.

Fish-scale tympanum, St. John the Evangelist, Pauntley

THE WALK

Leaving the church, walk in a westerly direction, back along the lane, bearing right at the narrow road. Onward - keeping a wary eye open for the occasional car - descending - passing Payford Pitch and Pauntley's village sign - over the River Leadon, and just beyond, taking the road left, to Murrell's End.

21

The road ascends to a T-junction with a bridleway opposite - you will see a blue arrow-head on a post. The gate is tied and bolted, but not impossible. On Shanks's pony, follow the track down the field - north-west - keeping to the route indicated by another arrow-head - a gap in the hedge - red mud underfoot, and the occasional nettle, to a small gate, along the edge of a field towards Cutmill. Gates are everywhere, these days - through another on your left to a lane, right for a few yards - gate, blue arrow-head - a short distance to a yellow arrow-head (dismount), where you turn right, as indicated, approximately north-east. Sheep, also, are everywhere - woolly baas - as you approach another gate and cross the field, still north-east. Part way along, by a right angle of hedge, stands, yes, you've guessed it - a gate and yellow arrow-head. Continue, still walking north-east along the middle of the field - Redmarley Woods to your right and a line of willows to your left. In the far right-hand corner is a gate which has to be climbed. Bear right, east, a bridleway - the imprint of horses' hooves in the ground. On through a last (almost) gate and further along taking the small gate to your right. This is a narrow track, boasting mud and nettles beneath a canopy of trees; coming, finally, to the road. Turn right, passing Laurentides, walking south-east, then go right at the T-junction along to Redmarley's Church of St Bartholomew. The church was locked - once, only, when I could not obtain keys. The entrance is on the right, the south porch. This door, too, can be 'difficult', but persevere. Walking along the nave - the brightly patterned kneelers catch the eye. On the north chancel wall is a rather battered brass to George Shipside (1609). Back along the north aisle - you should see Mrs Reed's cape in a glass case - around by the font - buried in the south-west corner is a 'Tombstone Survey'. One may also purchase a booklet by H. Morton Niblett which contains a history of Redmarley.

Back at the road, go left, passing the sixteenth century, timber-framed Church House, and further on, taking the road left, signposted Staunton. Paget Nurseries are at the corner - tomatoes ripening under glass. Continue along this narrow road to a gate on your left, opposite a very attractive, small thatched cottage. The footpath is signposted; in fact there are two - a pair of white, wooden walkers. Immediately through, take the gate on your right, avoiding the playing field, walking approximately east across the field to a small gate in the hedge. Bear right for about ten yards and then left, passing to the left of a house, across a patch of rough ground, following the path south-east to a stile in the corner. A yellow arrow-head with a black spot in its centre is on a post. Over and along the field, roughly east, to another stile and black-spotted yellow arrow-head. Scale, with 'style', walking south-south-east, now - the ground rises - you will eventually see the grandaddy of a disc and arrow-head high on a metal post. Strike across the next field in the direction indicated as far as the road.

Proceed along Innerstone Lane to a T-junction, turning right - another narrow road with a generous coating of mud - it ascends, curves right by Chapel Farm and eventually passes a 'semi-surfaced' lane on your left. You will see a small

DIY mail box on the corner. Don't pass - take this lane, west, through a gate with a red triangle in its centre, up and over a wobbly stile, ascending south, then descending to a stile in the right-hand fence. Move quietly and you may surprise the score or so of rabbits that were sunning themselves the last time I was here. A second 'stile wobble' and down, north-west, to a gate, then along an avenue of saplings sheathed in plastic - to a final stile and the road.

Left, here, a short haul over the river, retracing your steps - road (last ascent) and lane - back to the start of the walk. The seat on the south side of the church should still be there.

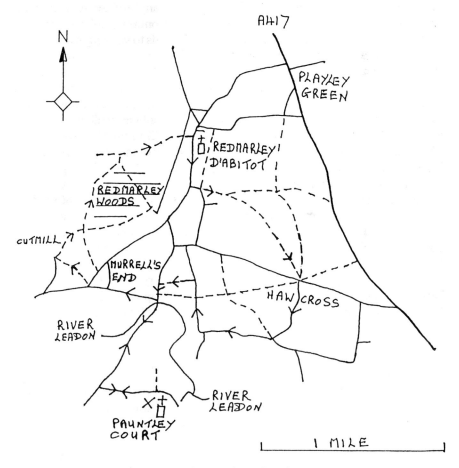

Pauntley and Redmarley

ASHLEWORTH AND HASFIELD

Two walks: one short (very), and one long (reasonably), only a few miles north of Gloucester. Low, flat country where, on looking at the Landranger map, the thin, blue line of the River Severn seems little more than a stream. In fact, it would require a long jump of truly Olympic proportions to cross. Both walks start in Ashleworth, close to the Tithe Barn [see *Parking*]. The longer one also takes in Hasfield by way of the river bank (no 'long-jumping' is necessary).

Route: *Ashleworth - Hasfield - Ashleworth.*
Distance: *From an easy mile up to 7 miles.*
Map: *O.S. Landranger 162.*
Start: *See Parking.*
Terrain: *Reasonable. Some mud, of course; but level.*
Nearest Towns: *Gloucester, Cheltenham, Tewkesbury.*
Access: *Junction 11 of the M5, A40, A417 (Ledbury) - through Maisemore, the village that thanks you for driving carefully, as far as Hartpury. Where the road curves left, just before the Royal Exchange Inn, take the road to your right, signposted Ashleworth. Narrow and winding - further along, go right, signposted (among other places) Ashleworth Quay, by the village green. A fourteenth century cross is here - stop to view if you wish, but it has become eroded with time. Further down, take the road, right, signposted Quay; this leads to the Tithe Barn and Church.*
Parking: *On the patch of grass beside the Barn.*
Public Transport: *The disused bus shelter is not very promising, but ring Gloucester County Council on 01452 425543.*
Refreshments: *Sink a pint in the Boat Inn.*

Suitably parked, boots at the ready, Ashleworth's Church of St Andrew and St Bartholomew beckons to the south-east. Through the churchyard - look up at the tower - gargoyles and a spire with a rooster on top. Several roosters of the crowing kind, parade opposite. Enter via the sixteenth century north porch. Inside, twentieth century lighting comes on automatically, then goes off as you leave - hi-tech. Walking to your right - past the nineteenth century font - on the west wall - the Lord's Prayer, Nicene Creed and Ten Commandments. Beneath the tower - various campanological feats are recorded on the walls, as are details of each bell: founder, diameter and date.

Returning east along the nave - in the north transept stands the church organ - raised due to flooding of the River Severn. On the east wall of the transept is a much worn brass to Sophronia Pauncefoote (1615). Pause before the chancel arch - you will see a Jacobean pulpit on your left and can look through a recently restored squint on your right - into the chancel which was rebuilt during the thirteenth century. The richly coloured stained glass in the east and north walls certainly catches the eye. There is a fifteenth century trefoil-headed piscina in the south wall and an Aumbry just to the right of the altar, currently hidden behind an arrangement of flowers.

Going right, into the chapel - the south window contains fragments of medieval glass - you can read the details yourselves. An ancient chest stands beneath this window. Walking west through the screen that separates chapel and south aisle - turn, looking back and up at a Royal Coat of Arms. The detail is none too clear - 'ER' above an English Lion and a Welsh Dragon. Notes on the Coat of Arms by Anna Hulbert, Restorer, are in the church booklet, which will also tell you that the south aisle, nave arcade and chapel are fifteenth century additions. Continuing west - another chest on the floor, and further, the usual Visitors' Book, the aforementioned booklet, and for budding cooks: a book of country recipes covering just about everything from soups to desserts, including a chapter on ciders and wines (but note St Peter's words which follow). On the west wall, you will see a Roundel. It dates from around 1700 and contains a warning quote: 'But the end of all things is at hand; be ye therefore sober, and watch unto prayer.' To mortalise: the door below the Roundel (behind the curtain) is called the Death Door. Read about it in the booklet.

Leaving the church - Ashleworth Court, which dates from around 1460 and is privately owned, is to your right - passing the porky pong of a piggery to the road where on your left stands the huge Tithe Barn. Built in the fifteenth century, and measuring 125ft. by 25ft, it is run, now, by the National Trust, being open from March to October. One may walk through and along - looking up at the queen-post roof trusses - some stone slates are missing - and out to the road.

THE WALK

If you have opted for the short walk, then here it is - an easy thirty minutes or so, that passes Ashleworth Manor. Go right, direction north, a matter of yards to where you leave the road, following a signposted footpath straight ahead. Further along, ignore the stile on your left: 'PRIVATE PROPERTY - NO ACCESS', continuing a short step to another stile in the corner. Over, then immediately left - north-north-west, give or take a degree - where a stile leads to the road. Turn right - passing, maybe, a 'fairly' friendly pint-sized dog with a gallon-sized bark, and timber-framed Ashleworth Manor. Also dating from around 1460, the Manor is privately owned, though according to the church booklet, may be visited by prior written agreement.

Continue along the narrow road, watching out for traffic at the blind corner, to a T-junction. Here, take the stile in the right-hand corner of the hedge (a 'two-stepper'), direction south-west, across the field to a last stile, still walking south-west, with the hedge to your right. Ahead, you can see the tower and spire of Ashleworth's church. Now, all one has to do is follow the line of the hedge back to the start of the walk, part of which has been done in reverse.

Feeling peckish? In September, one may pause for a juicy 'blackberry munch'.

Naturally there is an optional extra to this very short walk: nothing more than part of the long walk - as far along the bank of the River Severn as you care to go, bearing in mind that you will have to return. It is up to you.

The long walk takes in its stride: muddy mud, green grass, barbellate barbed-wire, chummy cattle (why do they always follow me?) and a car or three of road; quite pleasant, really. It continues past the Tithe Barn and through the floodgate, which forms part of a circular flood barrier surrounding the Boat Inn - to the River Severn. Here, go left, approximately north, joining the Severn Way Path. A long section, though briefly described: a succession of stiles, gates and footbridges alongside the river. Walking - a barge chugs by, 'V-rippling' through the water - one dozing sheep - I pass, close enough to touch, and have never seen wool move so fast. The Red Lion Inn stands on the far side. Surprise, surprise, the rain begins - men shelter under tent-like umbrellas, fishing, wetly.

Ashleworth and Hasfield

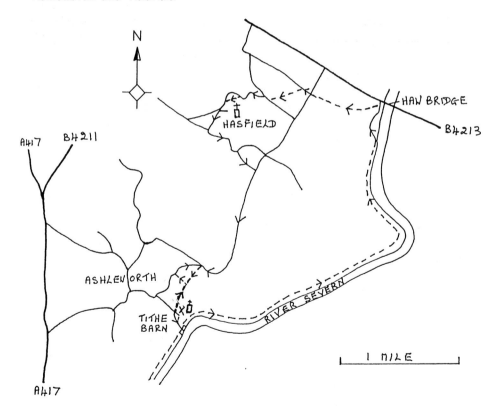

26

Finally, beyond the first house, bear left, slightly, along an unsurfaced lane - now tarmac - passing thatched Hazel Cottage and Withers Farm. Approaching Haw Bridge, you will see a signposted footpath on your left - over the wooden hurdle and along the field, north-west. The line of the path is trodden through thistles and grass - veering west, now, and at the corner of the field, go through the open gate, left a few yards - more thistles and grass - to where you turn right, over a ditch. You should see a yellow arrow-head with a black spot at its centre. Climb the wooden fence and on, moving closer to the right-hand hedge, walking north-west, to a stile beside a gate. An awkward climb (up and down) - thin walkers can even squeeze by. Continue, still with the hedge to your right, reaching a muddy soup (in wet weather), two more stiles and the road.

Proceed to the road opposite, signposted Tirley Hill; twenty yards brings you to yet another signposted footpath on your left. Negotiate a ditch and a couple of strands of barbed-wire with care, walking north-west along the field, sighting on a distant house. On through a dipping gap in the hedge, then across a last field to a gate with a hard spring-backed bolt that drops when opened - to - the road. Ignore the stile opposite, turning right - mostly tarmac underfoot from here on, and often 'mucky with it'. Mostly - beyond Primrose Cottage and another house (anon.), take the path across the field, direction west, joining and continuing left along the road, keeping left, signposted Ashleworth, as far as the telephone box. Opposite, is the lane that leads east to the Church of St Mary, Hasfield.

The church has origins certainly as far back as the thirteenth century, possibly the twelfth, and underwent restoration in the nineteenth century, when the north aisle and an arcade were added. The tower retains an earlier dedication to St Peter. All this and more, including details of the Pauncefoote Legend and parish links with America, may be gleaned from the church leaflet for a modest 20 pence.

On through the churchyard - its stubby tower is battlemented - exceptionally ugly gargoyles stare down. Around to the far side - half-way up the south face of the tower you can see a sundial. By all accounts, there is also a stone inscribed 'HW 1719', though I must admit to not seeing it. Enter via the timber-framed south porch, taking care closing the door which 'leans' heavily. The light switch is on your right, as is a list of Clergy from the year 1200. Going left, west, along the nave - passing the low, Norman, tub-shaped bowl of the font - under the tower arch; they take their bells seriously in this part of the county. Six curled ropes (the bells were installed in 1901) and a notice on the left-hand wall concerning the Incorporated Church Building Society (according to the dictionary, a sitting is defined as a church seat). A shield on the other wall records a campanological landmark.

Walking east along the nave to the chancel - the stained glass is, like that of Ashleworth's church, richly coloured; the east window is particularly attractive. In the far north-east corner stands the tomb of Dorothy Pauncefoote (1568).

One can still make out the inscription on its lid. Just above, a small brass plate tells you that the reredos and altar were erected by the Rev. F. Lillington in memory of Amelia, his wife. Strain your eyes and read it for yourselves - mine still ache from searching for that inscribed stone. Return via the north aisle, alongside the arcade, to the door and lane.

Continue left at the road, beside a high red brick wall, ignoring the road to your right, signposted Corse and Staunton, going straight ahead, signposted Ashleworth and Gloucester. It soon curves left around the grounds of Hasfield Court. Need I add: watch for traffic and keep to the grass verge wherever possible? Further along, before a line of houses (the first is called Rowan Cottage), is a signposted footpath to right and left. I prefer the road - passing what appears to be an abandoned bus shelter, and then straight on, signposted Ashleworth and Tirley, to a T-junction.

Turn right - plenty of grass verge - on past Colways Farm, home of 'The Hasworth Herd of Pedigree Holstein Friesians'. Quite a long stretch of road - steps to your right lead to the Meerend Thicket Nature Reserve and a lookout for twitchers (I think). The road traces a long curve around Stonebow Farm - careful at the blind corner - to a road on your left, signposted Ashleworth and Gloucester. This is the turning point of the short walk and offers two choices. One may take the stile (in the left-hand corner, now), part of the short walk back to the church (previously described). Alternatively, just proceed left along the road, past Ashleworth Manor, taking the stile on your left, retracing the first part of the short walk, and still enjoying an autumnal 'blackberry munch'.

A GLIMPSE OF GLOUCESTER

What to say? Where to begin? To describe Gloucester in a walking article is to attempt the impossible. Excuses, excuses; the best that I can offer is a 'mini-tour' of some of the many places of interest, and an optional stroll across 'pylonesque' Castle Meads and Oxlease.

They are relatively few in number, these places, but enough for most people, I think (hope). I will describe each, fairly briefly, 'en route'; for really, they form the first part of the stroll. The Cathedral, in particular, demands much research and a book to do it justice. Here, as with Tewkesbury, I can only touch the vaulted high (and cryptically low) spots, leaving the rest up to you. In any case, a Visitors' Guide and various leaflets may be obtained from the Cathedral Bookshop. Guided tours are also available; well worth taking advantage of, especially if one wants to see the crypt. I particularly liked the crypt (deeply interesting) and the Denny stained glass (transparently cryptic), which I will describe in a shade more detail.

To summarise: the 'walk' looks at the Folk Museum, the Beatrix Potter Shop and Museum, the Cathedral, the Regiments of Gloucestershire Museum and the National Waterways Museum. A relaxed wander of an hour or so follows, ending in Westgate Street's Car Park [see *Parking*].

Route: *A circular route within Gloucester.*

Distance/Time: *Difficult to estimate in terms of distance. An hour or so of 'pure' walking. You could spend the morning 'walking' in the Cathedral. Map: Not really necessary, but a freebie may be obtained from the TIC (see below).*

Start: See *Parking.*

Terrain: *On the level (honestly), apart from a few steps.*

Nearest Towns: *Cheltenham, Cirencester, Tewkesbury, Worcester.*

Access: *Junction 11 of the M5, and then the A40 into Gloucester. Follow the Cathedral signs.*

Parking: *Again, follow the Cathedral signs to Westgate Street's Long Stay Car Park.*

Public Transport: *Ring Gloucester County Council on 01 452 425543. There is also a railway station.*

Refreshments: *Aplenty, not forgetting the Cathedral's Undercroft Restaurant.* **Public Toilets**: *At your convenience: in the car park, the Cathedral, the Museums etc.*

The Cathedral: *For general information ring: 01 452 528095. Guided tours are freely available from late spring to early autumn. Outside these times, it is possible (if a party) by prior booking only. This is the only way to see the crypt (unless you are one of Beatrix Potter's mice or can call upon divine intervention).*

TIC: *The Tourist Information Centre, where one may obtain a stack of leaflets, is at St Michael's Tower, The Cross. Continue along Westgate Street to where the four main streets - North/South/East/Westgate meet. The TIC is on the far right-hand corner. Telephone: 01 452 421188.*

THE WALK

From the Long Stay, go south to Westgate Street, bear left and cross, making for the Folk Museum. An old, timber-framed building - see the lettering on the wall: 'Bishop Hooper's Lodging'. The Bishop was martyred for his Protestant beliefs in the sixteenth century - burned alive, according to the Museum leaflet. As with the Cathedral, entry is free, though contributions are gratefully received. The Museum is open all the year, Mondays to Saturdays, from 10 to 5; and from July to September, on Sundays, from 10 to 4. Get the green Museum leaflet and perambulate - upstairs and down. Many old crafts are on display (some are even practised). A small sample of what you will see is: 'tuppence-ha'penny' - two (non-decimal) penny-farthings, model GWR trains, jigsaw puzzles, mangles, a dairy complete with stuffed cow and cheese-making equipment, a Cotton motorcycle, heavy old irons - the 'detachable' sort that are left to heat up on - a kitchen range, not forgetting a photograph of the Severn bore - far from boring; in fact, very interesting.

A glimpse of Gloucester

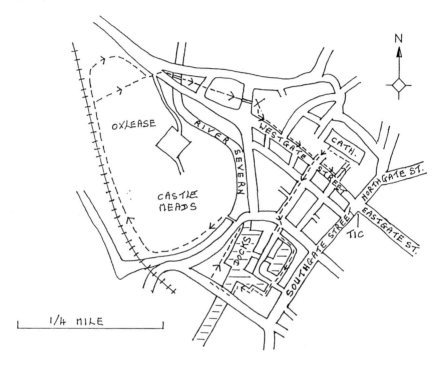

Leaving the Museum, cross the road and continue right, south-east, and where the road curves right, by the Old Crown, continue straight ahead, joining a welcome pedestrianised section, passing College Street and turning left into narrow College Court.

'Bespoke,' she said. On your left: 'The House of The Tailor of Gloucester', the Beatrix Potter Shop and Museum; home to Peter Rabbit, Jemima Puddle-duck and friends. Climb the creaking (squeaking) stairs - in the far corner is a working model of the sewing mice.

Back in College Court and continue to the end of the court - and there it stands - the magnificent Cathedral Church of St Peter, with its massively imposing (225 feet high) fifteenth century tower. Bear left, slightly, to the south porch. As previously mentioned, I can only briefly describe a few of the many features within. A guided tour is strongly recommended [see The Cathedral].

So, really, where to begin? Historically, with the founding of the monastery in 681 by Osric, Prince of Mercia. The numbers of monks and novices declined with the passage of time - advancing to 1022, when Benedictine rule was instituted by the Bishop of Worcester, and then skipping a modest fifty years to 1072 - a watershed - the appointment of the Norman Abbot, Serlo. This worthy recruited and began to rebuild. As the Visitors' Guide reveals, the foundation stone of the new Abbey Church was laid in 1089. Built mostly of Painswick, Cotswold stone (preferred because it hardens with age), the Abbey Church was dedicated to St Peter in 1100. And this, mostly, is what you see today.

Inside on your left is the Bookshop, where you may purchase the already twice-mentioned Visitors' Guide. Glossy and informative - an interesting read - why not 'take a pew' and browse? Just beyond the Bookshop, stands a statue of Dr Edward Jenner (the pioneer of vaccination), and behind and above the good doctor, the enormous west window. The Cathedral's stained glass (an acre or so), and the many effigies, tomb-chests, monuments and so forth are described in the Guide.

I chose, first, to go north, straight ahead, and right-angle around the cloisters. The fourteenth century fan-vaulting is very attractive - passing the Undercroft Restaurant and Cathedral Shop - the lavatorium where the monks used to wash their goose-pimples during the winter - into the garden for a look at the monastery well, coming finally to one or other of the cloister doors that lead to the north aisle.

Walking east - see the immense Norman columns that run either side of the nave. Entering the north transept - an opportunity (not always in the winter months) to visit the Treasury (which is free), and an exhibition of the Cathedral from Saxon times (which is not). In the former, one can only marvel at examples of the silversmiths' art. Back at the north transept - light a candle for ten pence, and continue around the ambulatory. You pass the tomb-chest of King Edward II: 'Murdered at Berkeley Castle on 20th September, 1327.' Dating from about 1330, the effigy is of alabaster, the tomb-chest of Purbeck marble. It is recorded that his burial was refused by the Abbots of Bristol, Kingswood and Malmesbury, but allowed by Abbot Thoky of Gloucester. An act both courageous and rewarding: further rebuilding was made possible by the offerings of the many pilgrims who visited the tomb.

On past the Lady Chapel at the east end - to your left, the entrance to what is called the South Ambulatory Chapel, though I believe it is now the Chapel of the English Saints. A visual feast, here, where one may admire the infinitely beautiful stained glass, 'created' by the Gloucestershire artist, Thomas Denny. Intensely subjective, and for a layman such as myself, not easily described. However, walking to and fro - the 'picture' changes with position and light and is open to different interpretations. It appears almost three-dimensional. Three windows of shifting colours, predominantly blue, flecked with yellows and greens. Look closely, and you can make out figures in the glass - the left-hand window - three small groupings near the bottom left corner. Other figures, or are they shadows? Maybe. A 'treescape', brightly yellow/green when the sun shines. The central window is clearer: the figure of Christ with a kneeling St Thomas to his right. The right-hand window - a shining moon or light at the end of a tunnel? A barred window with flaming orange beyond?

Ah, well, can't stay here forever - leaving the chapel, continue left, and then go right, into the presbytery. Beautiful hardly seems adequate: the carved wood of the misericords under the choir seating; the polished, coloured tiles in the sanctuary; the rare quadruple sedilia to the right of the high altar, even the scent of newly-arranged flowers.

Returning to the south ambulatory, continue west, entering the south transept. On your left is a red door - locked - the entrance to the crypt. Here, a guide of the two-legged kind is necessary, and, as with the Denny stained glass, my comments are superfluous, but who can resist? Take care down the steps to the original monastery and starting point of Serlo's rebuilding of 1089. 'Dem bones ...' the place used to be a charnel house - the bones were removed and buried elsewhere. Note the arches - reinforced on solid piers to cope with the tremendous weight bearing down from above. See, also, the moustached Norman heads carved in stone - a 'capital' effort. Essentially, the crypt is an ambulatory with radiating chapels: one such has a double piscina and (probably) the remains of a sedilia; another, is home to a huge Victorian font. The chapel windows are just above ground level - splayed - to allow the entry of maximum light. In the central area, water lying around the base of several columns attests to a high water-table; necessary, to keep the clay, below, from drying out. Your guide will explain regarding the three-centred arch. Up the steps, staying with the guide for the grand tour and/or leaving via the south porch.

Outside, walk south-west - along College Street, crossing Westgate Street into Berkeley Street as far as Longsmith Street. Here, bear right a few yards and then left by the Transport Museum (closed at the time of writing, but a peek through the window reveals an old Gloucestershire waggon), into Barbican Road. Straight on, ignoring the turning into Barbican Way, and at Commercial Road, take the pedestrian crossing to the Docks.

Inside, go immediately left, passing the Herbert Warehouse and the Victoria Warehouse, bearing left, around to the Regiments of Gloucestershire Museum. The Museum is open all the year, Tuesdays to Sundays and Bank Holiday Mondays, from 10 to 5. An eighteenth century soldier prepares to do battle at the front window. Brass band music and three hundred years of the military (and non-military) relating to the county's regiments. The Napoleonic Wars, the two World Wars and the Korean War are covered. But the Museum does not glorify war, other 'themes' are on display: art, crafts, documents, souvenirs, to name, gloriously, a few.

Continue, walking around the left hand side of the Victoria Dock - an interesting array of boats are moored, but watch your step - boats mean ropes - bringing a new meaning to a trip around the Docks. Cross the road and go (almost) straight ahead, passing to the right of the Docks Management Security Office. You can see (and read) the Llanthony Warehouse on the far right - make for that, where resides the National Waterways Museum, possibly even more interesting than the Regimental Museum and equally worth a visit. As the notice states: 'Three floors of entertaining history, working exhibits, special demonstrations, children's activity room, shop and cafe.' Open all the week in the summer, from 10 to 6, but ring 01 452 307009 in the winter. I'll leave you to splash around, unaided. Incidentally, the Docks get very busy in the summer months, particularly at weekends.

Warehouse and water, Gloucester Docks.

33

Leaving the Museum, bear right, south, mounting steps to Llanthony Road, and right again, crossing the narrow walkway of the bridge. Looking south, you can see the start of the Gloucester and Sharpness Canal. Beyond, turn right, back into the Docks, along the left hand side of the main dock, passing the Alexandra Warehouse. The Sailing Vessel Igesi Nagusia is currently available for charter. Cross two footbridges by two dry docks (full of water), walking as far as a lock. Here, continue to the left of the lock, ignoring the footbridge on your right. The Gloucester Antiques Centre is on your left. To the north, the River Severn splits in two, passing close to, and 'feeding' into, the Docks. It is interesting to watch the lock in operation. A boat enters from the river - low in the water - ropes are lowered and attached - water pours in and 'up she rises', bobbing like a cork. Continue north to the narrow but busy road. Cross with care by the bridge lights, taking the footbridge, direction north-west, over the river. This is the start of the stroll around Castle Meads and Oxlease which you may, of course, avoid by taking the ignored footbridge and retracing your steps back to the car park; first, perhaps, wandering some more around the general dock area. Water, water, every where ... what you have seen thus far may have 'wetted' your appetite sufficiently to go 'city walkabout'. At Westgate Street, you could turn right, as far as the meeting of the main streets, stock up on leaflets [see TIC] and really 'do the town'. I have only touched upon a few places of interest. There is much more to see.

So, to the stroll - beyond the footbridge, go left along the road for a few yards, and then left again, down steps to - this cannot be - but it is - grass at long last. Continue past some seats and tables (a picnic?) - you can still see the large warehouses on your left. Approaching an old railway line and bridge over the river, follow the path around to your right, past more tables, direction north-west, veering north.

Eventually, you (should) come to a wooden post, about two feet high - take the right fork. Further along, another post - this time, take the left fork. Continue, ignoring the signposted footpath to your left that dips under the railway bridge, reaching, finally, a high-stepping stile and a yellow arrow-head on a post. Up and over - Castle Meads Transforming Station is to your right - power lines and pylons go in all directions, but you walk past the rugby posts to fencing and a stile.

Two choices, here: the shorter route is not to climb the stile, turning right, north-east, initially with the fence to your left, across the field to a stile. Slightly longer, back at the fence and stile, climb and continue. The path traces a long curve to the right - north to east to south-east - to a gate and the notice: 'Over Ponds Nature Reserve'. This is where the two routes converge - a last gate, and over the minor road that leads to a car park, going east, across a patch of grass to a stile in the corner of a fence. The top of a post is painted yellow. Over, naturally, keep to the left, then left, through a gate, passing under one section of the busy A40.

Next, go right, south-east, along a footbridge over the river. The A40 is on either side. Beyond, bear left, slightly, across a patch of grass to St Oswalds Road. Cross with extreme care - traffic (one-way) whizzes by - you can see the Cathedral tower ahead. Proceed south-east, walking through the Westgate Galleria, a shopping centre. Sainsburys is on your left. You come to a second footbridge - up, along and down - back to the Westgate Long Stay and the start of the walk.

NEWENT AND UPLEADON

A short walk; a long walk; a look at Newent and Upleadon, all within the Gloucestershire Hundred of Botloe. Two interesting churches: a timbered Tudor tower and an armoured Tudor brass. The opportunity to visit a Victorian museum and ('off-route') the National Birds of Prey Centre [see A Wing and a Prayer]. The first walk takes in Upleadon only, while the latter includes Newent and will be described where it leaves and joins its shorter 'footmate'.

Route: *Upleadon - Newent - Upleadon.*
Distance: *Roughly 3 and 10 miles.*
Map: *O.S. Landranger 162.*
Start: See *Parking.*
Terrain: *Level with a touch of mud. Limber up beforehand; there are fences and gates to be climbed. Often, I have used roads - mostly quiet and narrow, but do keep an ear 'tuned' for traffic, using the grass verges wherever possible.* **Nearest Towns**: *Gloucester, Cheltenham, Tewkesbury.*
Access: *Junction 11 of the M5, A40 (Ross), then the B4215 - through Rudford, under pylons, eventually taking the road on the right at Highleadon, signed (a large rectangle) Hartpury and Upleadon. It is narrow - watch out for horses. At the crossroads by the War Memorial in Upleadon, bear right, along the road signed Upleadon Church, Staunton and Tewkesbury, and called Forge Lane. The lane to Upleadon Court (no signpost, though there is a sign in the hedge) is further to the right, beyond the Neighbourhood Watch Area sign.*
Parking: *Beside the Church of St Mary. Incidentally, you could base the walk in Newent or drive there separately to see the town. Unfortunately, it is busy in the summer when parking can be difficult. There is a small car park along Bury Bar Lane, to the left of the Market House.*
Public Transport: *I saw a bus shelter opposite the War Memorial in Upleadon. A timetable gave details of a few privately operated buses between Upleadon, Newent and Gloucester. There is probably a better service to Newent. Best to ring Gloucester County Council on 01 452 425543.*

Refreshments: *'Flask-it' in Upleadon. Aplenty in Newent. A Wing and a Prayer: The National Birds of Prey Centre lies about a mile south-west of Newent. It is open February to November, seven days a week; not included in the walk, however.*

Having parked [see *Parking*], St Mary's Church, Upleadon, beckons. With origins in Saxon times, the present church dates from the twelfth century. It was restored twice in the nineteenth century and again in 1969. A shiny, golden rooster perches atop the tower; similarly, St Mary's, on a mound of clay. This afforded a measure of protection against flooding of the River Leadon in earlier times, yet led to structural problems in later years. Mounting steps to the churchyard, why not a clockwise stroll around the outside? The north doorway is twelfth century - chevroned, with a sculptured Tympanum between arch and lintel - around and past the south porch (no entry), to the west tower. Dating from about 1500, the tower is timbered throughout and virtually unique of its kind. See (and feel) the massive timbers packed with bricks that line the walls. The tower forms an extension of the nave.

Through the north door - the font stands opposite - a selection of leaflets lie on a table, including a booklet which may be purchased for a mere fifty pence; treat yourself. The Black Letter Bible is in a glass case, nearby; details are in the booklet. Going west, 'inside' the tower - the curved bracing timbers catch the eye, as do the four tie-beams and king-posts in the roof of the nave. Walking east along the nave - past the pulpit whose oak panels date from 1661 - into the chancel. Now look back - above the chancel arch - see the carving of the head of a pig? This, too, is described in the booklet.

THE WALK

Leaving the church - down steps to the lane - go right, direction north, to the road. Left, here, past the Neighbourhood Watch Area sign, taking the third signed footpath on your left - south - over the stile, across the field keeping the wire fence to your right. Climb the wooden fence, and you are at the end of the lane that runs west from the church. Next, go immediately right - another climb - over a red gate, fielding west, the hedge to your right - on through a gap in the hedge - a field to a stile and the road.

Turn left - in name, not a road - Middletown Lane. Plenty of grass verge - 'zedding' the Z-bend through Middletown, passing Middle Town Farm. The road ends at a T-junction. Bear right, as indicated by the signpost that reads: 'Upleadon and Pauntley'. Further, ignore, if only doing the short walk, the road to your left, signposted Newent and called Hook's Lane. Ignore, also, the first two signed footpaths to your right (one has a 'branch-stile'). Onward - the grass verge - 'traffic-wary' - soon reaching a signed footpath on your right, close to a: 'Forest of Dean District Council Mini Recycling Centre'.

Go right, along this path, initially a lane, direction approximately east - climbing the wooden fence and walking across the field, the hedge to your right. Avoid the stile in this hedge, scaling another in the right-hand corner to a triangular field. At the far end, the ground dips to a stile, where you go left to the road. Bear right, back to the start of the walk.

Newent and Upleadon

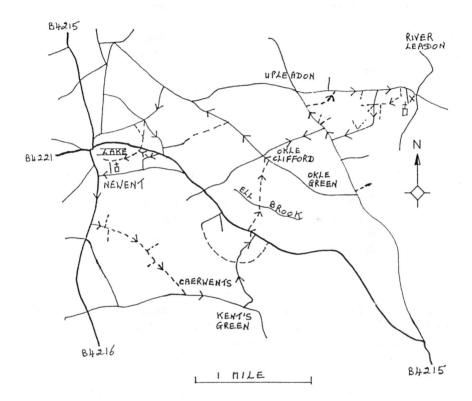

So, to the long walk, which I will describe from the previously ignored Hook's Lane on your left, signposted Newent. Turn left - a narrow, metalled road - on past Cowslip Bank - Gadling - Five Oaks, and bearing right at the crossroads, signposted Dymock. Northcote House is on the corner. Continue - just beyond Appleyard Cottage, you come to a T-junction, where you go left, signposted Newent and Dymock, joining the Newent-Upleadon road. A shade busier, this, so watch for traffic, using the wide grass verge wherever possible.

On past Sherworthy, which offers picture framing - the tasty sign: 'Strawberry Hill' stands by the hedge, following the main route past Plumtree Cottage. You may have realised by now that this is a fruit growing area, a fact reinforced by much glass of the non-stained kind to your right. Inside, strawberries in pots ripen in the sun.

Bear left where the glass ends - the road narrows and descends, passing the entrance to Poykes Farm and Cleeve Mill. Under the B4215, and further to the right - a twenty-first century moonscape? Well, a couple of futuristic domes set in a grassy wasteland; soon to be houses and shops, no doubt. Go right, approximately north, making for the domes - currently, one is a veterinary centre, the other, empty. Walk between the domes, along a path, direction west, entering a wooded section. Two or three paths, here: just keep moving in a general westerly direction, across several footbridges. Keep to the left of the watery reflections of Newent Lake, and at the far end, veer left, making for the Church of St Mary, Newent. You should see the spire through the trees.

Timbered tower, St.Mary, Upleadon

Upon reaching the church - time for another clockwise stroll, noting the battlemented north side of the nave, around to the south side (also battlemented), past the small timbered porch to the main entrance - the porch beneath the tower. The sun shining on the sundial on the south-east corner of the tower casts an accurate shadow (no second-hand, though).

St Mary's has undergone much alteration-restoration-rebuilding during its 'stormy' history. The tower is fourteenth century. Tower and spire are 153 feet high overall, with variations. 'Stormy history ... with variations.' Intrigued, I am sure that you will want to know more; a booklet, inside gives the full details. To summarise: the spire was 'seen off' by a high wind in 1661. Eventually rebuilt, all went well until a 'large crack' appeared in 1968. This time, the church had to be closed. The top of the spire was restored in 1972. Similarly, the nave - in 1674, it collapsed under a ton or so of snow, and was rebuilt during the succeeding five years.

Enquiries revealed that the church is 'generally open' though there have been problems with theft and vandalism. In case of disappointment, ring the Rectory on 01 531 820248 or Church Office on 01 531 821641.

In the porch stands an Anglo-Saxon cross shaft which is believed to date from the ninth century. On through the door - the seventeenth century font stands just to your left. Plenty of leaflets, a Visitors' Book and a booklet for reference only. At the time of writing, a Mark Two version was 'due out soon'. I went straight ahead to the north-west corner, a glass case and the Newent Stone. A little on the not very large side. As with the cross shaft, it is pre-Conquest - notes on display give the detail.

Walking east along the nave, past the seventeenth century pulpit and entering the chancel - the organ, with its beautifully carved organ case, dating from about 1740, stands to your left. On the east side of the organ are several interesting newspaper extracts - June 1737 - from the Gloucester Journal. The stained glass of the east window is very attractive. A framed key to this window hangs on the north wall. Facing south, note the two pointed arches separating chancel and Lady Chapel - the arches are thirteenth century. Beneath the left-hand arch is a fourteenth century tomb-chest and effigies of a Knight and Lady, the Knight enjoying a canine footrest.

Squeezing by the tomb-chest, into the Lady Chapel - lying against the east wall is a slab with a brass to Roger Porter (1523) - eighteen inches of Tudor armour. Set in the south wall is a fourteenth century piscina, and above, another stained glass window. You can read the dedication at the base. Hardly ancient or outstanding, I suppose; yet I particularly liked the colouring and detail. Turning west - as you leave the chapel, on your right is a list of Incumbents from 1301. Look, also, up at the flat, wooden ceiling to the two massive seventeenth century windows above the gallery at the far west end.

In fact, there is a lot of clear glass all around - the church is very light and roomy inside. Finally, as you leave, a framed photograph of St Mary's as it was in 1905 hangs on the wall to left of the door.

Leaving the church, go south to Church Street - the Post Office is opposite. Turn right, passing The Shambles: 'A museum of Victorian life'. It is open from March to December and closed on Mondays (except Bank Holidays). Crossing the street - you should see a Council Office which offers a stack of leaflets covering Newent and the Forest of Dean area. Continuing - past the timber-framed Market House - traders still sell goods beneath its supporting posts. Follow Church Street where it winds into Broad Street as far as the fish and chip shop - 'timber-fried' with 1465 on the front. There is a Tourist Information Centre in the library that lies further along Broad Street.

At the F & C, turn left - Culver Street, eventually passing the Wesley Chapel, a barn, clearly dated: 'H.B. 1695', and Tan House, which is late seventeenth century. The sign: 'NO FOOTWAY FOR 250 YDS' needs no explanation - proceed with care - the road narrows - pavement once more - a seat: '...in memory of Edith Curtis ...', for the use of the residents of Highfields rather than walkers - approaching Cherry Bank and Connemara Close, and opposite, to the left, a signposted Southend Lane.

Take this lane - walking - it's like being in Essex - Southend House, Southend Nurseries. By the house, Southcote, the lane loses its tarmac surface, and after about thirty yards, you should reach a stile on the right and a gate on the left. But you go straight ahead, a point south of east - an arrow-head on a post directs around to the right and then ahead - a muddy path - along about a ten-yard strip of no-man's-land - soon emerging onto the right-hand field.

Nearby, a farmer ploughs a lonely furrow or two, attended by about fifty seagulls. News of a free lunch travels fast over the air waves. Turn left, with the hedge to your left, mostly maintaining a south-easterly direction from here to the road. Follow the arrow-heads - a second field - a short distance to two posts with arrow-heads - one points left - follow the other, ahead, still in this second field, at the end of which you should see two arrow-heads and a 'path diverted' notice. One points to the right, the other, ahead, bringing you to an adjacent third field - field number four - a grassy lane, passing the farm buildings of Caerwents - to - yes - an arrow-head on a post which guides around to the right and on to the road.

Bear left, east, making for Kent's Green, and then left again, signposted Newent - the house Tall Trees is on one side. This road takes you past Vine Cottage (holly packed with red berries - a hard winter to come) and Upper Orchards, ending at the B4215.

Cross with care, going left for about forty yards to a signed footpath on your right. When walking this section to Okle Clifford, keep mainly a degree or two

40

east of north. Over the stile across the field to a footbridge, then a second field to a rickety old gate (a wobbly climb). Around a soggy patch of ground to two gates, either side of a small bridge over the Ell Brook. Happily, both gates open, walking alongside the brook - stile-railway sleepers-stile - another field, passing to the right of a water trough (lumpy ground), through a gate and farmyard to a stile. Up and over - the stile at the far end of this field opens to a small triangular patch of ground, somewhat overgrown. Trail-blazing - scale the stile in the corner, moving immediately right, the hedge to your right, to a last stile and the road. Go left at the road, and right at the crossroads, back along Hook's Lane, finally joining the short walk (even retracing the first part), as previously described.

CHURCHAM AND BULLEY

A walk around Churcham and Bulley within the Hundred of Westbury. You will see a spire with a difference, visit Henry Hook's grave and admire centuries-old wall paintings. I have tried to tailor the walk to the situation at Bulley; a key move is necessary [see *Church Key*].

Route: Churcham - Bulley - Churcham.
Distance: A minimal 4 miles.
Map: O.S. Landranger 162.
Start: See Parking.
Terrain: *Level with a dollop of mud. There are fences and gates to be climbed.*
Nearest Towns: *Gloucester, Cheltenham, Tewkesbury.*
Access: *Junction 11 of the M5, A40 (Ross). Passing the Churcham village sign - a little further, on the right-hand side of the road, and pointing left, you should see the signpost: 'Churcham Church'. Left, here, along Church Lane. It is small and can easily be missed, given that one cannot dawdle along the busy A40. In this case, continue as far as the lay-by [see Refreshments], and return.*
Parking: *At the end of Church Lane, opposite the church. Public Transport: I saw two bus stops: one in Churcham and the other in Birdwood, along the A40. Ring Gloucester County Council on 01 452 425543.*
Refreshments: *There is a 'takeaway' in the lay-by west of the entrance to Churcham Church.*
Church Key: *At the time of writing, St Michael's at Bulley is kept locked (vandalism). 'Designer walking' - with this in mind, obtaining the key and visiting the church is included as an option during the walk. Woodgreen Farm, the nearest 'key point' is not too far away and fits in reasonably well with the route. If no one is in, two other places are mentioned 'in passing', but they are further away and make the walk 'awkward' (a separate drive, perhaps?). The church is worth a visit, however, even if only to view from the outside. As a last resort, try the Reverend Jenkins on 01 452 750252.*

41

Having parked [see *Parking*], the Church of St Andrew, Churcham, stands to the west. On through the lych gate - ducks tread water on your right - following the path around to the left-hand side of the church. The oddly-shaped spire catches the eye - past several tombs covered in ivy, and an old font, to the south porch. Before entering, you may wish to go south, along to the graves of Ada and Henry Hook - 'Hookie' of Zulu fame. 'ALFRED HENRY HOOK, V.C. ... IN MEMORY OF HIS HEROIC SHARE IN THE DEFENCE OF RORKE'S DRIFT, NATAL, 1879.'

With origins in Norman times, St Andrew's underwent some rebuilding in 1878 following a fire two years earlier. Inside the porch, you will see traces of a wall painting - twelfth or thirteenth century - a splash of red on the arch above the door. Entering - the modern font has an inscription at its base: '... A GIFT IN MEMORY OF EDMUND WRIGHT ...' Walking east along the nave looking up at the slightly 'skewed' and restored chancel arch - on your left, an organ of 'parts' - pedals and keys in the nave, pipes in the chancel, with a conduit of cables joining the two. In the chancel, the stained glass east window behind the altar is quite attractive, as is the nineteenth century panelling in the sanctuary.

Leaving the church, go right, west, for a closer look at the spire: unusual in form and name - Rhenish helm - and very rare in this country. Birds are a problem, so I was told; their droppings tend to rot the wood. Install an avian loo, I suggested, to an unsympathetic audience. Walking around to the north side - set above the arch of a doorway, a foot or so of sculptured stone, reputedly third century.

THE WALK

Returning to Church Lane - by the lych gate is a footpath sign that points west (beyond the tower). It is shown on the Landranger map, but is less than ideal. A stile opens onto a 'ploughed prairie'. Many of the old hedges have gone.

So, at Church Lane, go left, direction north, to the A40. Cross with extreme care, taking the lane opposite - a crumbly surface - on through two gates. A third gate by some farm buildings has a 'pistol-grip' bolt that is difficult to close. Continue, still north - a bridleway - to a 'bridle-gate', doubly closed by binder twine and chain (remember for later), and straight across the next field, forever north. In late autumn, winter wheat is poking its head above the ground. At the end of this field, a blue arrow-head on a post directs along a country lane, emerging onto the edge of a field. A last gate brings you to the road.

Turn left - forty (measured) paces - on your right is a 'fence-stile' Climb and continue, direction north-north-west, keeping the hedge to your right of the hedge that points in the same direction.. In the far corner - another 'fence-stile'. Over and along, to a proper stile this time. Over (naturally), following the line of the path (about ten yards from the hedge), ascending, walking north-west, now. The path eventually veers north to a post covered in arrow-heads, where you bear left, west, continuing as far as a metal gate, which opens to a larger than large field.' Strike south-west across the field to a stile close to a water trough. A yellow arrow-head points the way to the road.

Churcham and Bulley

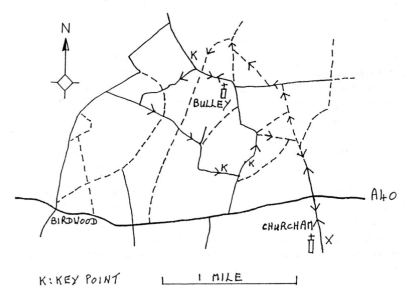

K: KEY POINT   I MILE

Opposite, is a Neighbourhood Watch sign, and at this road the option of a 'there and back' visit to Bulley's church [see Church Key]; otherwise continue as described later. Really, St Michael's should not be missed.

To the church - bear right at the junction, signposted Tibberton, walking the short distance to Woodgreen Farm. Try the bell at the side entrance. Key in hand, return to the junction and go left along Bulley Lane. Watch for the blind corners. Further along, a gate opens to the churchyard. Ascending - no tower or Rhenish spire, a nineteenth century bell-turret, then around to the south porch of the Norman Church of St Michael, Bulley.

Keyed up and ready? You will not be disappointed; the church has much to offer. The doorway, for example: dogtooth decoration and chevron mouldings, with a plain tympanum above the lintel.

Inside, the font has a Norman bowl; the small table supports a Visitors' Book and gives one the opportunity to purchase notelets and Bulley tea-towels. There is also a small framed note giving some church detail. Walking east along the nave - around the two Norman windows in the north wall, traces of twelfth century wall paintings - red - chevron pattern. Approaching the chancel - freshly

43

modern - a fine display of chrysanths (sorry, long gone by the time you get here) - the pulpit on your left, and above, on the north wall, a tablet: 'UNDERNEATH THIS PLACE LIETH THE BODY OF JEREMIAH HOOPER OF THIS PARISH WHO DIED DEC 24, 1763 AGED NEAR 67 YEARS'. The chancel arch has two orders of chevrons, which are most attractive. The chancel was rebuilt in 1886, and as a result has a rather 'new' look about it. Five simply-patterned, yet engaging stained glass windows run along the east and south walls. There is also a 'modern' sedilia on the south side.

'Rhenish helm' spire, St. Andrew, Churcham.

Stating the obvious, lock the door, retrace your steps to Woodgreen Farm and return the key. Back at the road junction, take the road on your right, signed Lake Lane and Birdwood, direction west. Continue, always 'car-wary' (cars tow caravans to the farm, a Caravan Club site). Bear left at the T-junction, signed Churcham - a right-angle - a 'left-angle' - passing, on your left, the bungalow 'Littlefield' [see Church Key] and a signed footpath that crosses the road. Approaching the T-junction - on your right, is the bungalow 'Windana' - no key, but a very helpful lady and gentleman who fed me coffee, biscuits and information, all gratefully digested.

At the junction, ignore the path opposite, turning left, signed Bulley and Tibberton, passing Mayfair, in particular, number four [see Church Key]. Onward - just beyond Mayfair, ignore, also, the signed footpath to your right, going as far as the 'semis'. One is called Carpenters Cottage. Here, take yet another signed footpath to your right, walking across the field, approximately east. Oil-seed rape is showing; hopefully, the tyre tracks will leave a path in the summer. On through a gap in the hedge, continuing east, ignoring the right-hand stile. Does the area look familiar? Remember the 'bridle-gate'? Well, unless lost, you should see it on your right, and can begin to retrace your steps back to the start of the walk.

MITCHELDEAN AND ABENHALL

A look at two St Michaels and a choice of two walks. Not so much eights to figure or circles to circulate - loop-the-loop walking. Loops one and two, around Mitcheldean and Abenhall, with a roadside view of the hill fort in Welshbury Wood and passing the remains (though little remains) of an old blast-furnace. Enjoy the woody views and fairly easy, though possibly muddy, walking.

I had hoped to park at pivotal Abenhall and describe a figure of eight - north-west to south-east. Unfortunately, Abenhall's church is kept locked. Keys may be obtained from St Michael's Rectory, Mitcheldean, which is passed during the walk. At the time of writing, it is only feasible to borrow the key if doing the first loop, a walk of around forty minutes, plus church browsing, say thirty minutes. The second loop adds another fifty minutes, leaving the Rector (and other walkers?) 'keyless' for two hours; unless you are Superwalker. Rumour has it that 'new people' in Abenhall may be persuaded to keep a key. When this happy day dawns, only the 'key borrow' need change; Mitcheldean's car park is better than Abenhall's grass verge and narrow road.

Route: *Mitcheldean - Abenhall - road junction near Welshbury Hill Fort - Mitcheldean.*
Distance: *2 or 4 miles.*
Map: *O.S. Landranger 162.*
Start: See *Parking.*

Terrain: *Level with a smidgen of mud.*

Nearest Towns: *Gloucester, Cheltenham, Tewkesbury.*

Access: *Junction 11 of the M5, A40 (Ross). Just beyond Huntley, take the A4136, left, signposted Monmouth. On through Little London and Longhope, entering Mitcheldean. At the mini-roundabout, take the right-hand road (third left) signposted, in various places, Newent and Ross. This is the B4224, along Merrin Street, Hawker Hill - you will see the spire of Mitcheldean's church, ahead. Straight on past the George Hotel into High Street.*

Parking: *Motoring along High Street, you cannot miss the Car Park sign just past the library, where you turn right into Brook Street. It is small, so get there early. There are toilets on one side.*

Public Transport: *Ring Gloucester County Council on 01 452 425543.*

Refreshments: *The George Hotel, the Lamb Inn and a fish and chip shop opposite the library.*

Library: *In Mitcheldean's High Street, offers a raft of leaflets and a browse. Newly built and open Mondays, Thursdays, Fridays and Saturdays*

Flaxley Footnote: Nineteenth century (rebuilt) St Mary's Church (which is open) and twelfth century Flaxley Abbey (generally not open to the public) lie about a mile south-east of the road junction near the hill fort. The Abbey, in particular, has an interesting architecture and history: founded for the Cistercians in 1148 by Roger, Earl of Hereford, in memory of his father, Milo Fitzwalter, reputedly killed by a stray arrow when hunting in the forest on Christmas Eve, 1143. Neither are included in the walk, but don't let that stop you; watch out for arrow-heads, though.

Having chained the chariot [see *Parking*], go through the pedestrian arch to the left of the back of the library. Cross to 'Ye Olde Mitcheldean Post Office'; further, on your right, stands the Church of St Michael and All Angels, Mitcheldean.

Tall and tapering, the impressive eighteenth century spire pierces the sky. Entering the south porch - beneath the tower - eight bell ropes hang loosely curled. A description of the bells is on the right-hand wall.

Another door - inside, stands the richly decorated font with the figures of the Apostles on its sides. A list of Rectors from 1280 is on the left-hand wall. Turning to your right - leaflets; currently, the church leaflet is out of stock. A reprint is due, though there are 'board notes' for reference. On the right-hand wall are the Baynham brasses: Margaret (1477) and Alice (1518), the two wives of Thomas Baynham, who died 'brassless' in 1500. A few yards beyond, at the end of the wall, is the seat taken from the fifteenth century pulpit situated to the right of the chancel entrance. Walking east along the nave - look up at the clerestory and fifteenth century roof - panels plastered a light blue.

Miners' Guild Stone, St. Michael, Abenhall.

Moving to the south side, along the south aisle, the entrance to an ossuary and a priest's door. Regarding the former: the 'bulge' on the outside wall hides a spiral stair from the rood loft downwards - a repository for bones dug up in the churchyard. Also in this south-east corner is a fourteenth century piscina.

At the entrance to the chancel - a wooden screen with the carved figures of Christ and several angels - 'All Angels' - there are angels everywhere. Standing back a little, look up at the fifteenth century painting - in oils on oak - Christ, and below, eight panels depicting various times in his 'life' ... Before Pilate through to The Resurrection. On either side of this entrance: the aforementioned fifteenth century pulpit in the shape of a wine-glass (a peek inside shows where the seat used to be), and a wooden canopied pulpit.

Entering the chancel - the sanctuary was rebuilt in the mid-nineteenth century (when the church was also restored). The white marble reredos, which dates from 1911, really catches the eye - the words: 'COME UNTO ME' - and life-sized - Christ the Healer surrounded by the sick. The east window, behind the altar, is by John Hayward and dates from 1970 - modern stained glass, also with angels 'on high'.

Leaving the chancel, go right, passing a stand for votive candles (light one), coming to the north side. The 'Rosser' brass, complete with translation, is on the north wall. And then back along either of the two north aisles, admiring the finely-carved, fifteenth century oak roofs (more angels). One really needs to get at the light switches to appreciate the detail, though with the electricity bill in mind, I did not dare. Finally, to the south porch and away.

THE WALK

Back at the pavement - in Mill End are several timber-framed houses, part modernised, part original, which date from the sixteenth century. Turn right, along High Street, passing the George Hotel - High Street becomes Hawker Hill. On your right is the entrance to St Michael's Rectory where you may borrow six inches of key that fits the door of Abenhall's church. The last time I visited, they had discovered a well in the garage - drop in, any time. Continue down Hawker Hill, into Merrin Street, and at the mini-roundabout, cross to the Lamb Inn, taking the road opposite, signed Flaxley and Westbury-on-Severn, appro-priately named Abenhall Road. Keep to the right-hand side, leaving the road for a footpath - ascending - nearing the top, a pavement begins, and where the road curves right, by Dene Magna School, cross to the signed bridleway, direction east, veering south-east. This is reasonable walking apart from a scattering of brambles and nettles. Approaching a narrow and often mucky road, go through the 'railing-gate', up the churchyard, to the Church of St Michael, Abenhall.

With origins in the thirteenth century, St Michael's more than repays the 'miner' inconvenience of obtaining the key; as with Bulley, another key move. First, walk past the south porch, to the west side. Set in the west wall of the tower is a Miners' Guild Stone, a sculpted shield - picks and spades - together with the head of a Free Miner wearing an archer's cap. The original stone has been replaced by this replica, the work of a local mason, Mr Dennis Russell. There is a photograph of him 'putting finishing touches' in the Miners' booklet.

Booklets - inside, the opportunity to purchase a booklet which describes the church much better than yours truly; and also another booklet: 'The Royal Forest of Dean - Free Miners' Association'; an interesting read for a paltry pound. There is usually only one on display, so snap it up. Money in the sweet jar, please. Immediately to your left, stands the font - octagonal - fifteenth century - see the shields on its sides, and read all about them in the booklet(s). Walking east along the south aisle - on the east wall is a list of Rectors from 1307 and more 'framed' church detail. Returning to the font, go under an arch of the fourteenth century arcade to the stained glass in the west wall: 'IN MEMORY OF FRANCIS LLOYD 1824-1905'. Walking east along the nave - more stained glass in the north wall - past the stone pulpit, into the chancel.

The north chancel window contains fragments of fourteenth century glass with, as the framed notes state: '... fine flowing tracery ...'. This glass reputedly shows the head of St Catherine of fourth century Alexandria. Legend has it that she was martyred on a wheel for refusing to give up her faith and marry the Emperor Maxentius. The wheel broke and she was beheaded. St Catherine is the patron saint of those who work with the wheel; hence Catherine-wheel. Looking back at the west window - it improves with distance. In fact, dare I say: there is much attractive stained glass all around. Beneath the carpets on the floor of the chancel (front centre - lift with care) is a brass to Richard Pyrke (1609), his wife Johan, and their two sons.

Leaving the church, locking the door and pocketing the key, go south to Church Lane, and then bear right, west, past The Old Rectory, as far as the junction. Ignore, if doing the first loop, the signposted footpath to your left, turning left (in fact, straight on) along the road. Negotiate the blind corner with care, taking the signed 'PUBLIC PATH' on your right. Continue down the track, the hedge to your left - a muddy wallow in wet weather, to a gate which, when lifted off its catch, drops alarmingly. This is the entrance to a sort of 'gate pen'; four gates in total. The one opposite, with the arrow-head, is entered from the south-west when ending the second loop and joining the first.

Here, take the gate on your right (unsigned). It has a spring-backed bolt, and the gate must be pressed down before it can be opened. Walking approximately north, now, a ferny hedge to your right, and at the end of this field, climb carefully the bare essentials of a stile - and on - mud and rubble underfoot, then a grassy path, direction north-north-east - another stile and yellow arrow-head - watch out for the bramble overhang - descending - the surface becomes almost cobbled. Ignore the signed footpath on your left - ahead, you should see a stretch of tarmac, the end of a road - not too many yards before this road is a signed footpath on your right. Nimbly, up and over the stile, walking east - ascending - easing - making for the gate just to the left of Dene Magna School. At the road, go left along the pavement, retracing your steps (not forgetting to return the key), to the start of the walk.

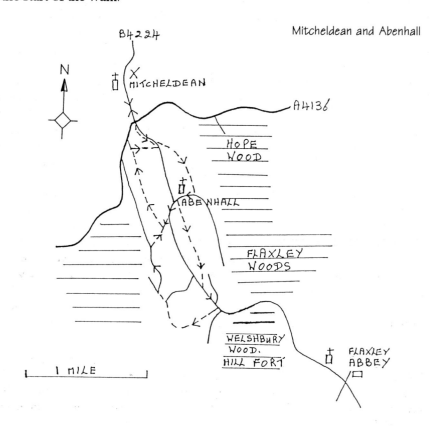

The second loop leaves the first at the end of Church Lane in Abenhall. Instead of bearing left at the junction, take the signed footpath on your left, south-south-east. A gate surrounded by mud, and held fast by chain and twine (not as bad as it sounds, but be sure to close - cattle make for the milking parlour through here). Down the field, through a gap in the hedge (more mud), a second field, still south-south-east. In the corner of this field, climb a 'fence-stile', moving closer to the stream - a wire fence on your left, down to a gate with a yellow arrow-head on a post. A lane leads to the road.

Turn left along this narrow road, always 'traffic-wary', and at the junction, pause to look up at the Iron Age hill fort in Welshbury Wood. Inaccessible from this side (blame Ramparts Anonymous - hill forts were not designed with

50

hospitality in mind), though there is a path up to it further along the road signed Flaxley and Westbury on Severn, towards Flaxley Abbey.

Continuing the second loop, take the (initially) unsurfaced lane, opposite the Flaxley road, direction west. Tarmac - on past Gunn Mill House, an indication that on your right lie the (hidden) remains of an old blast-furnace. In the seventeenth century, some of the guns cast here were used in the Royalist-Parliamentarian Civil War. No rusting cannons pointing skywards, I'm afraid; this is a walk that also exercises the imagination. Entering a wooded section, past a notice: 'NO ENTRY TO UNAUTHORISED VEHICLES'. Walkers - OK. The lane loses its coat of tarmac, curving west to north. In late November, bare wood, patches of holly and a red/brown leafy carpet draw the eye, especially when lit by a pale sun that laces through the trees. Tarmac again - leaving the woodland - one or two houses, dogs, even a couple of goats. Approaching the school, ignore the signed path just before, but take the one just after, that points right - north-east. A strip of pasture - a second stile plus arrow-head - and on, still north-east, across a field to a gate that opens to the previously mentioned 'gate pen'. Fortunately, it opens easily, where you then take the gate on your left, the one with the similarly previously mentioned spring-backed bolt, joining the first loop back to Mitcheldean.

RUARDEAN RAMBLE

Ruardean sits high on the northern edge of the Forest of Dean; a small town, yet large, historically: during the Civil War, Ruardean, being ideally placed for guarding the Forest's north side, was made a Parliamentary military post. The all-important iron - and those plundering Cavaliers from Goodrich, whose castle was eventually taken by siege. Shoot/Shots/Shooters Hill lies behind the Malt Shovel Inn [see Refreshments], under which (so it is said), is burrowed a square tunnel, probably used as a store during the War. Cannons on Shooters Hill, where numerous cannonballs have been found.

A very brief history, by way of introduction, and a choice of two main walks - long and short. You will visit an interesting church and traverse much attractive woodland, especially so during the spring. Ruardean Hill, the highest point in the Forest, is scaled (easily), affording magnificent views; except during the short walk, when you will have to be content with almost equally fine views to the north-east. Also, during the long walk, you will get your first look (so far) at the River Wye - distant, only, but there will be the opportunity to splash around during later walks; perhaps a summery swallow-dive at Symonds Yat.
No doubt, by the time I get to the south side of the Forest, I will have long since run out of adjectives to describe the scenery which throughout is stunning in the extreme. An arboreal thesaurus 'wood' be useful.

Route: *Ruardean - Ruardean Woodside - Ruardean Hill - paths/road to the north of Ruardean - Ruardean.*
Distance: *3, 5 or 8 miles.*
Map: *O.S. Landranger 162.*
Start: See *Parking and Church Key.*
Terrain: *Not too bad; an ascent or ten, several possibly 'frost-slippery' metal stiles, a shade muddy underfoot in places.*
Nearest Towns: *Gloucester, Cheltenham, Tewkesbury, Ross-on-Wye.*
Access: *Junction 11 of the M5, A40 (Ross). Beyond Huntley, take the A4136, left, signposted Monmouth. On through the suburbs of Little London and Longhope, entering Mitcheldean. Go straight across the mini-roundabout, ascending Plump Hill - the road dips and twists like a ride on a roller coaster - about two miles further, take the B4227 on your right, signposted Drybrook and Ruardean. If you should journey via Lydbrook, watch for the hairpins.* **Parking**: *Entering Ruardean, along High Street - there are no 'proper' car parks, so one must improvise. I parked along School Road which lies opposite the church. There is just about room for four cars (if three go elsewhere) beside the toilets.*
Public Transport: *I saw several buses, public and privately operated. Ring Gloucester County Council on 01 452 425543.*
Refreshments: *Drink: holy, from the Angel Inn; hoppy, from the Malt Shovel Inn. Jack's Chippy along School Road, reopened after a two-year lapse Duberley Stores sells various edible goodies and is also a sub PO. The Masons Arms, passed during the long walk.*
Public Toilets: *Further along High Street, bearing left off the main road by Duberley Stores, which is opposite the monkey-puzzle tree.*
Church Key: *At the church, go left, east, along High Street. Cross by Church Villa to the Rectory (a bungalow) which stands back a bit, just beyond a red brick terrace. Keys may also be obtained from No. 1 Norman Way, which is off School Road. A Thank You: I would like to thank Mr Andrew Gardiner, author and local historian, who kindly allowed me to 'rummage among his grey cells' for Forest snippets; and Mrs Gardiner for the welcome cup of coffee.*

Inventively parked [see *Parking*], obtain the church key [see *Church Key*] and make for the Church of St John the Baptist, Ruardean. St John's dates from the early twelfth century and was restored in 1890. The spire, in particular, impresses with its flying buttresses and crocketed pinnacles. The rooster, too, is something to crow about - to set a picture puzzle: without scaling the spire, how can you get a closer look at him?

First, a clockwise stroll around the churchyard - to the north, you can see the remains of what was at one time a castle. Reputedly, there is a tunnel between the church and these remains. Along the tarmac path - there are many old Forest tombstones against the walls.

Back at the entrance to the south porch: on the left, stands (again reputedly) a Roman altar - about 3 feet high. (The Romans were certainly in possession of Gloucestershire from around AD 40 and mined iron in the Forest.) Above, is a sculpted head, and in the porch, between the arch and lintel of the door, a Norman tympanum depicting St George and the Dragon (as with the rooster, a picture puzzle, but more of that later).

Inside - the plain yet ancient font - '1657' is on one side. On the south wall to your left is a carving of two stone fishes. You can read all about the discovery of the Pisces on the notice below. Further along the same wall is a plan of the church as it was in 1884.

Threading east down the south aisle - a 'picture' of The Last Supper - a tapestry: '... in loving memory of the Penn family of Ruardean', and also framed church detail which tells you that: '... the tower with its 180-foot spire was added in 1365 with flying buttresses added in 1866 ... renovated in 1974 ...'

At the Lady Chapel, go north, passing under an arch of the thirteenth century arcade - a face on the right gives one a rather stony look - entering the chancel - on the south side, the blocked up rood-loft entrance (mind the one step) and a thirteenth century piscina. On the north side, deep in the sanctuary coal mine, a lit (electric) Davy Safety Lamp. Leaving the chancel, going west along the nave, past piano and organ - the carved wooden panels of the seventeenth century pulpit are a rich, dark brown. On the north wall, 'ye olde' lettering: 'HEERE LIETH ENTOMED THE BODY OF JOHN HANKINSON ... 1637'. By the entrance to the tower - a bell and box requesting donations to the bell fund - feel free to ring the changes, large or small. Thou shalt not trespass - a quick inspection of the area beneath the tower (which may or may not be allowed) - curtains and door. Inside, eight bell ropes, Tierceron vaulting, and much interesting photographic church history. For example: an aerial photograph of the church, bell ringers ringing, a close-up of the rooster (picture puzzle solved), a list of Rectors and Curates from 1777 and the tympanum painting.

From the tower, walk back along the nave, and then towards the south porch - passing the Visitors' Book and (at the time of writing) being asked the question: 'Would you like to make and donate a kneeler?' An excellent example is on the table; almost irresistible, but only if you are good with needle and thread.

THE WALK

And so, to the short walk. I assume that you have seen the church and are standing outside, boots poised, raring to go. Turn left, direction east, along High Street, returning the key (cross and back again), on past Ruardean Village Hall to where the road curves right, making not so much a turn, as a continuation, left, off High Street, along Varnister Road. Pavement and then grass verge - bungalows on either side, going straight ahead by the 'bung', Cinderberry, to the road junction and Varnister Lane.

Here, take the signposted footpath opposite - a short stretch of unsurfaced lane - after a night's heavy rain, river-like and inches deep in mud. At the gate (dog on a lead, please), negotiate the metal stile with care. A word of warning about such stiles: treat with caution when icy, risking numb fingers by gripping the posts and top rungs. Over and across the field, keeping the hedge to your right, walking in an easterly direction. Another metal climb, and on, ascending slightly, mounting more metal, the hedge to your left, now; still ascending - to where the ground levels and the hedge angles left. Remember this spot, you will 'sight on it' upon your return. Continue east - you can see a house in the distance - over a 'fence-stile', along a narrow tract of grass (the long walk joins from the right) and climbing a 'hurdle-stile'. The house is opposite. I will call this the 'walk crossroads' for later reference.

Go left, walking in a northerly direction, and where this lane curves right, continue ahead through the gate and on to a post covered in arrow-heads (6 at the time of writing). Again, ahead, the wire fence of the field to your left - descending - veering north-east - over a stile to the road.

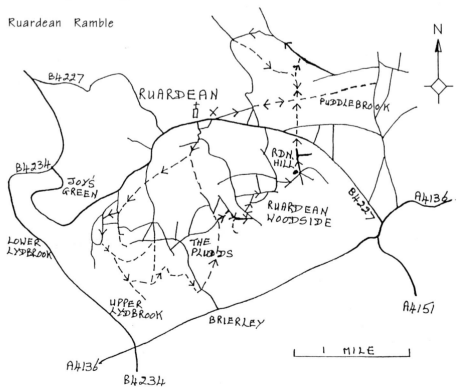

54

Turn left, west, along this narrow road. It is fairly traffic-free, with some grass verge, but take care - descending - trees on either side - steeply - later taking the left fork, signed Ruardean and Howle Hill. A couple of ascents and a scattering of houses brings you to the junction.

Here, leave the road for the stile by the gate on the left-hand corner, just past the entrance to High Stones. An arrow-head directs - walking south-east across the field, the hedge to your left, as far as a post with two arrow-heads, going through the gap in the hedge to the bordering field, and then bearing right, the hedge to your right, this time; undulating, for want of a better word. Climb the next 'stile' with care - there may be a wire fence (non-barbed) on the other side. It is easily stepped over - to a muddy syrup in wet weather. Straight ahead - negotiating gaps in fences, 'stiles' and fields - trees start to appear on your right - passing soggily by a stone shed - cows chew and stare - hello there. Keeping fairly close to the trees, you come to a last gap in a fence (an unhinged gate lies on one side). Beyond, stands the previously-mentioned post - one of its 6 arrow-heads points right, south - easier walking, retracing your steps to a point near the house by the 'walk crossroads' referred to earlier. This is where you go right, over the 'hurdle-stile', pausing to take a bearing, west, to the remembered corner. From time to time, you will see the flying-buttressed spire of Ruardean's church, as you return to the start of the walk.

You may prefer the more convenient Norman option [see *Church Key*] before starting the long walk. As ever, you have seen the church and are standing outside, hooks-a-tenter. Return the key (of course) and proceed along School Road, opposite. Further, bear right, off the 'main' road, but still along School Road, and then leaving it, ascending Kingsway Lane, as far as Pettycroft. Here, take the signposted footpath, approximately south-west, almost straight ahead. You come to a gate that is tied to, and extends beyond, two posts. Climb and on, with the hedge to your right. Roughly two-thirds along, take the 'fence-stile' on your right, walking south-west, again; the hedge to your left, now; an adjacent field. Nimbly leap over the stile in the left-hand corner - the faint outline of a path and another stile brings you to the road.

Bear left for a few yards and then take the 'signposted' bridleway (currently, the post is there but the horse has bolted) on your right. Still south-west - a wide, unsurfaced lane, somewhat muddy in places. Cutler walking: the lane ends at a road, where you 'pick up' the right fork, opposite Patch Cottage - on for a few yards, this time selecting the left fork. At this 'V', pause and admire the view below: watery and woody; the River Wye lazily 'horseshoeing' around the valley. Continue down the road, passing a telephone box, eventually reaching the Masons Arms - tempting - for the mason's wife, perhaps; it's up to you. Just

St. George and the Dragon tympanum, St. John the Baptist, Ruardean

past the MA, where the road curves right, turn left along a track, direction east, veering south-east, entering Ruardean Woodside. Further along, leave the track for another on your right. The former curves east to north, the latter continues south-east. A reasonable surface, this; one that would easily accommodate a car, yet reveals the imprint of horses' hooves and a boot or two. The track winds a bit, up and down, but is pleasant enough walking. Descending - really, one cannot see the wood for the trees - conifers, broadleaves, patches of broomy Cytisus and prickly green gorse. The track is joined by another - onward,+ keeping left, yet ignoring the wide track to your left, following the main route, which also curves sharply left beyond the ignored track - winding gently down - levelling - coming finally to the road.

Turn left over the small bridge and then right, north-east, tracking again. Two streams converge and enter the pipe under the bridge. Later, bear left - a path/ bridleway which runs nearly parallel for a while - overhanging conifers and an unusual 'eye-level' view along the 'forest' floor. Pining for an ice- cream? There
are many cones lying on the ground. Ahead, you will see a few houses and part of a road, but take the footpath to your right, over the stream, ascending, and ending at the back of a house where a semi-surfaced lane begins. A short, stiff climb brings you to the road. Pause to get your wind back and admire yet more stunning views across the tree tops.

A section of road walking follows: some pavement, some grass verge, nothing at all in places, so watch for traffic. Turn right along the road, south-east, passing a school - not a bad place to spend one's childhood - a forest for a playground. At the junction - a 'proper' road, with central white lines, where you bear left, signed Ruardean, again passing what turns out to be Ruardean Woodside Primary School, walking along Brierley Road, as far as a bus shelter where Brierley Road ends and Ruardean Road begins. Turn right, direction east, signed Ruardean Hill, ascending Forest Road, following this road - up, down and around - past glass, paper and tin banks - coming, at long last, to a flagpole marking the highest point in the forest - 932 feet. Flagstaff Cottage is on one side. View of views, here; a panorama of trees and rolling hills.

The road walking section ends as you take the lane, direction initially north-north-west, veering north, passing to the right of: 'RUARDEAN HILL BEA-CON PAN TOD'. A tarmac surface begins - curves right - just beyond the detached house is a signposted footpath on your left - and a 'fence-stile' with a (possibly) slippery wooden step. Over with care, down two fields to the road. Straight across - another 'fence-stile' - another road. Again, straight across - a narrow path between house and garage, still north. Approaching the house by the 'walk crossroads', scale the 'fence-stile' on your left, continuing to a point roughly level with the house, where you join the short walk. Two choices: left, returning to Ruardean; ahead along the short walk, both previously described.

CHURCH-GOING

INTRODUCTION

As most of my walks include a church or two, I thought I would attempt an article on the subject. A few words by a layman for laymen, 'laywomen' and 'laychildren'; certainly non-academic, non-definitive and probably 'non-error-free'. I hope that you find them of some use in your ecclesiastical wanderings.

Basic church diagram

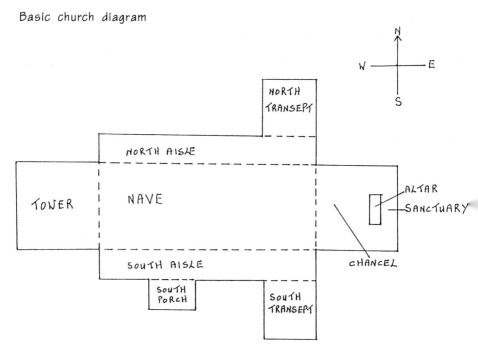

PRAYER-BOOK

Churches are 'stored history'. They record the lives of the communities that they serve: from major social upheavals to a death in the family; from past centuries to the present day. Approach a village church ... it may appear bypassed, set apart, hardly relevant to today's world. But take the time and trouble to investigate further ... people actually worship there, meeting are met, fetes are feted, funds are funded. Churches are built to last, and they do (unlike most other buildings). Architecturally, they are unique - going back through time - care to seek and ye shall find an immense variety of interesting things: traces of bullet holes (marks of the Civil War), a Norman tympanum, a Saxon cross, wall paintings, beautiful stained glass, 'rubbable' brasses ... the list is (nearly) endless.

PRAY IN AID

The Church of England is in retreat. It owns much land and property (commissioners control around £3 billion of assets), yet there seems to be relatively little in the way of liquid assets (Severn flooding excepted). A mind-boggling £800 million lost in property speculation in the 1980s does not help. Attendances, too, are falling; hence the 'Flying Vicar', where more than one church is 'served' by an Incumbent. Some churches have been closed and sold, others 'retired', being used only on special occasions. In my churchly wanderings, I have canvassed the opinion (vicariously?) of quite a few Incumbents: one or two, inevitably, may be described as dog-collared dinosaurs; the majority are more realistic, realising that the church has to adapt to survive - shorter services at more appropriate times, for example, and talk of signs of revival. Please bear in mind when visiting that the cost of upkeep is horrendous (a modest contribution is not too much to ask). There are also problems with theft and vandalism. I have come across churches that exist in a state of siege, particularly those in and around densely populated areas. Of a necessity, they will be locked. The same can apply out in the country, where the walks are walked. In most cases, keys are obtainable.

NORMAN KNOW-ALL

And now, for those with Catholic tastes, a word about architecture and so forth. Compacted geology - you will often read of a church being described as Saxon or Norman, fifteenth century ... or whatever. Maybe, but not always - what you may come across is a site on which stands a church: possibly originally built of wood (of which nothing remains), and then perhaps replaced by (another) Saxon church (of stone, that has mostly gone), on which has been built a Norman church, which in its turn has been altered and restored several times in subsequent centuries. One just cannot think in terms of black and white - it is Norman or it is not. Throughout the centuries, funds are started and met - work is done - and you end up looking at a 'mix' of various styles - a jigsaw puzzle, and unless you are an expert (which I am not), it can be somewhat confusing.

Although one cannot draw a line - there is overlap - certain periods give rise to certain styles; and, of course, the above slightly simulated pearly words of wisdom are not always true. So, what to do? Grab a kneeler and pray for divine assistance? But you do not have to be 'church literate' to appreciate the detail; there are usually leaflets/booklets within, which may be purchased for a few pence. Gloucester and Tewkesbury have bookshops. As a last resort, cast a critical eye over my efforts - briefer than brief, pointing the pinnacles - for walkers, en route.

CHURCH STYLES/PERIODS

From the 7th to the 16th century (C), with just a few of the features typical of each period. Really, the subject is a specialist one and requires a lifetime's study.

Saxon (7C to 1066). An almost severe simplicity of style - pre-Conquest. *Long and short work* - describing the use of huge stones through the corners of the walls. *Pilaster strips* (a pilaster is a column that projects, partly, from a wall). Small, rounded windows and 'basic' towers.

Norman (1066 to 12C). The transition to *Gothic* architecture, and a period of considerable church building executed on a much larger scale, particularly towers, arches, columns and piers. The introduction of chevrons, tympanums and vaulting.

Early English (Gothic) (late 12C to late 13C). The pointed arch, high lancet windows with occasional tracery, and more attention to the decoration of towers. **Decorated** (Gothic) (late 13C to late 14C). As the name implies, richly decorated in general: spires with crockets and pinnacles, the buttresses of towers, slender arcade piers, vaulting. Larger windows with ornate tracery.

Perpendicular (Gothic) (late 14C to mid 16C). Lofty, elaborate towers. Vertical window-tracery. Fan-vaulting, panelled walls and still larger windows.

The **Tudor** style lies at the end of the Perpendicular period. For walked examples, see the armoured Tudor brass in St Mary's, Newent (as well as a Saxon cross), and Upleadon's timbered tower.

And beyond ... well, **post-Reformation** (*see below*) and not described here.

A FEW DEFINITIONS

Aumbry - a recess for church vessels. *Battlement* - an indented parapet or wall. *Chancel* - the eastern end of a church that contains the altar (see *diagram*). *Chevron* - a zigzag moulding. *Choir* - where the church choir sit, usually at the eastern end of a church. *Crocket* - additional decoration - to pinnacles and spires, for example. *Nave* - the main part of a church, but excluding the chancel and transepts (see *diagram*). *Pinnacle* - an ornament, usually conical or pyramidal in shape, that adorns a spire or tower, for example. *Reformation* - the sixteenth century religious movement that gave rise to the Protestant Church. *Reredos* - an ornamental structure of wood or stone behind the altar. *Rood* - the cross or crucifix (figure of Christ on the cross). *Rood Screen* - the screen that separates the choir and the nave. *Rood Loft* - the gallery over the rood screen. *Sanctuary* - that part of a church around the main altar. More generally, a place of refuge from persecution. *Sedilia* - a recess in the south side of the chancel with seats (usually three) for the priests; singularly, a sedile. *Squint* - an opening in a wall that permits a view of the altar. *Stoup* - a receptacle for holy water. *Transept* - the transverse section of a cross-shaped (*cruciform*) church, ie, the part (where it exists) that lies at right angles to the nave (see diagram).

GETTING THERE
... AND HOME AGAIN

INTRODUCTION

A little light reading - cautionary - to be taken with a pinch of leather wax in the comfort of your home - planning and preparation, getting there, walking and browsing, and getting back again.

PREPARATION

What to take? Food and drink: economy DIY, a dip into Refreshments, supping en route, or even waiting until you get home. A shade extreme, perhaps, but a toilet roll in the boot as a last resort. Brambles can scratch, so stick in a plaster or two just to be on the safe side. Maps (road and walk) - the Landrangers and Pathfinders give more detail, though there is a sketch map with each walk. A compass - cheaply purchased and sometimes useful when, perish the thought, you take a wrong turn and follow a path that fades into woodland.

What to wear - clothes (pedestrian humour), 'covered' in the Introduction, proven boots - and whatever you do, don't forget the waterproof (with a hood). I usually carry one - rolled - which also doubles as a seat while admiring the view. When to go walkabout - whenever you can - weekends, probably, but don't forget the cool summer evenings. Mid-week in the autumn is my favourite time. Why not invest in a long range weather forecast and take a week off? Far better than roasting, browned-off, in Spain. Prolonged ecstasy is a crisp day, a blue sky and a (barely) warm sun. Agony is sitting in the car while the rain bounces off the roof.

GETTING THERE

How: usually by car, possibly by bus (unfortunately, not that easy, 'farely' expensive and time-consuming), and rarely by train. See the prologue to each walk.

An unwelcome embrace - in the long arms of the law - for speeding or being (even a point) over the limit are the twin nightmares of the road. The police are unsympathetic. Not only that, nowadays, the poor old motorist has to grapple with technology - speed cameras on bridges, for example. The fine arrives in the post.

For whom the road tolls; it tolls for thee, motorist. Ringing the changes across the Severn Bridge: free from Wales to England at the moment, while a second bridge is now with us, bringing with it the horror of two-way, two-bridge, automatic electronic tolls. And the result is - a lot of people take to the A roads, lorry drivers included. Gnawing one's knuckles while 'convoyed' in traffic does not add to the overall enjoyment of a walk. Most of my walks go the long way around - junction 11 of the M5. This avoids a stinging toll, but is more expensive in terms of time. These are only possible routes. You may prefer to work out an alternative; it depends on where you live, really. The problem is - everything changes; and cost, as ever, soars.

In many respects, one enters an unreal world when motoring the motorway lanes. Behaviour and perceptions alter: speed, particularly, increases as you glide along, cocooned in your metal shell, master (or mistress) of all you survey. Good intentions - an initial benign hover on seventy - may be forgotten when a lorry whizzes by in the outside lane. Cones, contraflows and road works lurk; traffic crawls, blood pressure rises. Unnecessary risks may be taken (a backseat driver may even be a help). Reality is leaving the motorway.

WALKING AND BROWSING

Walks change with the seasons: trees that are green, tinted or bare; hard ground that is now a muddy soup; wet, knee-high grass that can appear almost overnight; crops to be negotiated; 'skiable' stiles, and the motor car. Always watch out (by ear rather than eye) when walking the narrow roads. There are dogs, too, barkers and non-barkers, ferociously woolly sheep (not really), and cattle 'deposits' that don't do much for the leather of one's boots. This is part and parcel of the walking experience; yet there are compensations: blackberries and hazelnuts, for example, freshly picked and very (very) tasty. Unless you have granite teeth, the nuts are best left to home and the nutcrackers. Conker players will find plenty (in season) on the ground.

As mentioned in the Introduction, physically, walking is about stamina, and unless experienced, it is wise to pace yourself. Second and third winds later, put the legs on autopilot and get the most from the day.

What to look at? What to look for? Everything: foxes that do not bother to pleasantly pluck pheasants, and plenty of other wildlife, numerous churches (try counting the crosses on the Landrangers, or standing on high ground in places and counting the towers), hill-forts, and many other places of interest. You will find that Gloucestershire is blessed with an almost infinite variety of the viewable.

Walkers/visitors may just want to drive somewhere, look, wander for half an hour or so, then drive back. Which is fine; amend the walk accordingly. Alternatively, there are those who count their pleasure in miles clocked (I know of several who turn their noses up at anything less than 15 miles). Again, fine; combine and/or extend, though bear in mind that you will have to get back again. Linear walks, in particular, pose problems.

.... AND HOME AGAIN

Briefly, getting there in reverse, when you may care to consider a different route, and also give some thought to the Monday to Friday rush hours. The one thing that sticks in my mind when returning via the A48 to the Severn Bridge is (in the sun), the scintillating Old Course Hotel - a final sparkle to the walk

CONCLUSION

I hope that the above does not seem too banal, irrelevant, pessimistic, or even ridiculous; its purpose is to help you get the most out of walking in Gloucestershire. Walking, next to swimming, is the best exercise that you can get - exercise with compound interest added - better, if you want a truly unbiassed opinion. Fill your lungs with (hopefully) fresh air and enjoy the countryside. There are places to see, people to talk to, and dogs to be barked back at. Walk the same walk at different times of the year; challenge yourself by walking the walk in reverse (not backwards); and consider - there are only 9 more to go!

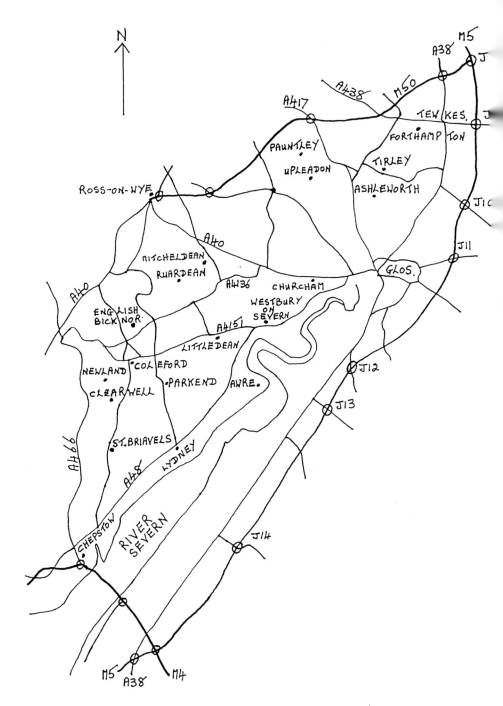